SEARCHING FOR EDEN

Helen Cottee

Dedication…

This book is dedicated to the brave souls who will not stay still or silent when they feel the call to something more.

'What if you find yourself stuck in a story that no longer fits you, and a life that no longer works? What do you do? Where do you begin to sort it all out, and find your way through? Begin here, with this book. *Searching for Eden* is a compassionate, practical guidebook for all of us who long to remake our lives but aren't sure how to begin. With compassionate vulnerability and practical wisdom, author Helen Cottee shows the way.'

Michael Warden
Leadership Coach
Author of 'The Transformed Heart' and 'Leading Wide Awake'.

'If you talk to anyone who knows Helen well, you'll quickly pick up some of the themes which run through her life. A deep desire to be authentic, to be honest about her own struggles and to create space where others can be honest about theirs. A big heart, always looking to share whatever she has that could benefit someone else. A positive vision for how life could be, believing that our future doesn't have to be defined by our past or our present. And an ability to create safe places where people can grow together, both through mutual learning and by allowing God and his truths to permeate every area of our lives.

All of those themes seem to come together in Helen's latest book, *Searching for Eden*, born not out of just a set of ideas or theories but out of her own life journey. I pray that through it many of us will be able to move towards the better future God has for all of us.'

Simon Benham
Senior Pastor, Kerith Community Church, UK.
Author of 'The Peach and the Coconut'.

'Helen Cottee is a moving communicator, both in spoken word and written. She has a gift for taking simple, and usually very humorous, stories and magically turning them into a gold mine of learning. Dive deep with her into this journey to Eden and enjoy!'

Lisa OBrien
Life Coach & Spiritual Director.
Author of 'Reflections on the Twelve Steps: A Companion to Freedom'.

Acknowledgements…

My Kick-ass Editors: Thank you for being so much more than editors, thank you for being my friends, my encouragers, my inspiration to keep going. Thank you for holding me to my best and for kicking me when I needed it. There are few people who can pin me down whilst lifting me up. You have done both so beautifully.

My Girls: You know who you are. Thank you for helping me to taste and see what Eden can be like - the space you created for me is the inspiration for this book and the work I do in the world. Thank you for showing me what true healthy community is like and the difference it makes to the world when you find and create it.

To Dave, William and Megan: this is for you. You have my heart. I pray I can be the best I can for you before anyone else, to offer this to you first. Thank you for being my home.

CONTENTS:

	Hi!	Pg 11
	Prologue: Road Blocks	Pg 15
1	Welcome	Pg 21
2	Introducing Eden	Pg 29
3	Around The Evening Fire	Pg 33
4	Tell Us Your Story	Pg 39
5	Let The Renovation Begin	Pg 47
6	Beautiful	Pg 55
7	Pioneer	Pg 67
8	The Green Blob Of Connection	Pg 77
9	Come Out Of Hiding	Pg 85
10	Finding Your Voice	Pg 93
11	Your Skirt Is In Your Knickers	Pg 101
12	Stuck in The Middle With You	Pg 109
13	Stop and Celebrate	Pg 121
	Epilogue: Find Your Tribe	Pg 127

Hi!

However you ended up with this book in your hand, I'm pleased that you have. I'm pleased that I get to share my thoughts and my heart with you about the amazing journey I have been on over the last few years in the pursuit of 'home' - the places and people with whom I can be myself, find acceptance and feel deeply loved. I welcome you to explore some of the ideas I have pondered over; I welcome you to wonder about this metaphor of 'Eden' and what it means for you now and moving forwards as we seek to build lives in which we are thriving and fulfilled.

Let me sum up for you the main idea of this book: we all search for places and relationships which are healthy, fulfilling and life-giving. The image of 'home' gives us an amazing picture of what we hope to find, whether in our actual homes or in relationships where our heart feels like they have found 'home'; the places where we belong. We all know that most of these spaces in our worlds, families work places, friendships are far from perfect and so we feel this yearning for something greater, better, more fulfilling - we may call it perfection. I have called it 'Eden' because Eden was the place of paradise where those first lucky people got to set up home and experience a type of thriving relationship that our hearts still seek.

This book is an invitation down a path that I have been intentionally walking as I have searched for 'home'. It is presented to help you as you walk your path, to find the universal similarities - the same potholes and road blocks, the same longings and hopes - whilst recognising that your path is unique and will look very different from mine. My greatest hope is that by the end of this book you feel like you have some tools in your hand to help you build something new in your world. These tools are ones I have practiced and developed; some of them may be new to you and some may be familiar. As you try out these tools, remember that when things are new and unfamiliar it can be hard to know what to do with them and you can feel a little uncomfortable wielding new tools for the first few times - that is quite normal! This book will help you to practice using tools that build relationships, create deep connections and bring change - no one expects you to use them perfectly or competently to start with, although you may surprise yourself along the way.

Some of you may find that this work goes to deep places within you. Great! When we go to deep places, we find deep levels of hope and freedom. You may find that you want to invite someone else into those places with you if that's helpful. I find the help of a good friend, mentor or small group invaluable - in fact so much of this work has been walked out for me in those places.

I am also a passionate believer in the use of professional coaches and counsellors for certain parts of our journey. Welcoming someone else into the process is an amazing step. If you feel like you need someone to step onto the path with you as you make this journey, please get in contact through my website. I'd love to help you to journey in a way that works best for you.

And trust yourself. A good friend told me that 'in the walking we find truth…'. As you walk out the ideas in this book you will discover things about yourself and those around you - others can help us to put words and edges to those newly explored places but you will know better than anyone what you desire, hope for and need - so trust yourself through this process and trust yourself as you go to new ground.

Something you should know about me is that I am passionate about change. I believe in our ability as humans to grow and develop. I worked for several years as a qualified behaviour teacher and I loved offering children and young people tools to help them change in ways that created more life in and for them. Now as a life coach I am still as passionate about offering tools that help bring change. Too many people stop growing and learning when they leave school, they get caught up in the 'doing' of life. The great sadness is that there is always more to learn, more to explore, more new ground to find, if only we carry on with a mindset that welcomes and seeks change.

This material invites change because it seeks something different. This is a search for something else, a yearning for something more - and you become the agent for change in your world as you walk out what it looks like to thrive.

The book is structured in a way that tells my story of the path I have walked, explains concepts and tools that supported my journey and then invites you to explore your own path that you are walking. You will find these three things woven through the book so allow me explain them in a little more detail:

1. Ideas and concepts: There are lots of different ideas in this book that are the tools to help you to build this home we have called 'Eden'. There are tools offered around concepts like change, vulnerability, finding your voice and expressing your needs. I explain these ideas and offer ways you can practice these ideas in your current relationships - at work, in your family, in your church, with friends… you get to choose where you would like to explore something new. You may choose to try these tools out in several different places. Amazing!

2. Story: I have peppered these ideas with my story to explain some of the journey I have been on. My story is not perfect, I am not setting myself up as the example to follow, I am simply sharing my heart around the 'home' I desire to build in my world. Story is the beautiful living evidence of the places we have been and I hope that my story will be an encouragement to you as you are walking out your story step-by-step.

3. Journal time: Because your story is different to mine, there is a lot of space for you to journal your ideas about how the concepts in this book relate specifically to you. In these spaces you will get to try out the tools, you will get to practice them and see what they feel like in your hand. It may be that very quickly you feel comfortable enough with that tool to try it out in real life - you may start a new conversation with your spouse or child or boss. It may be that writing something down on the pages of this book is a bold enough step at the moment. The journalling pages help you to give these things a go without an audience whilst you build up the confidence to use them in your actual day-to-day.

I heard a talk by a clinical psychologist called Dr Roger Bretherton this week. He was talking about change and he said something I really, really love. He said 'if something is worth doing, it's worth doing badly'. If you desire something new in your life, it's worth trying it out before you know that you can do it perfectly. No one runs a marathon the first time they put on a pair of running shoes. So allow this book to be your practice arena. Put on your running shoes and take a few faltering steps, and then a few more. I will cheer you on as you do, shouting encouragement from inside the arena as we try to run this race well.

I believe there is a place we are each able to dream of and imagine, where we are thriving and fulfilled, and I believe that we get to create these places one small step of change at a time - one kind word, one thoughtful deed, one brave conversation, one well placed 'yes' or 'no'. Perfect homes are not built overnight, but it's amazing where you may find yourself when you practice putting one foot in front of the other.

Here's to the journey; the steps towards the dream of what could be.

Helen x

PROLOGUE:

ROAD BLOCKS...

change that is more than skin deep

There is much scientific research into cell regeneration and it's fascinating stuff if you're into all that… I recently heard that scientists estimate that our skin is completely replaced and renewed every seven years - totally new, totally changed. Of course, the truth is that our bodies are constantly in the process of change - always in the middle of regeneration. Your skin does not suddenly get left behind like a shedding snake on your seventh, fourteenth and twenty-first birthdays - that would just be gross. Your skin changes through a daily process of brushing off the old dead cells in order to give way to the new life-filled ones.

Change is a normal process which shows growth and development; it is a sign of life. The only time your body will stop regenerating is when it is void of life. Whilst you're breathing, you're changing.

We are unaware of our skin changing because it just happens without any thought or mindfulness - our body simply gets on with the process of change; every day replenishing, replacing, renewing. If your body is healthy and able to progress as it was intended, it will keep on changing day in and day out. We are unaware because we can be unaware; unlike the process of soul change. This process is not so easy. You cannot stop your body replacing itself, but you are fully capable of inhibiting your heart, soul and mind change. If we want to change the internal stuff, we cannot take the same stance of unawareness that we do with the changing of our skin - internal change requires intentionality.

We've all come across people who seem to be incapable of, or unwilling to, change. They do the same damaging or irritating things over and over. There are people who just never seem to learn - they go from job to job, relationship to relationship, exhibiting the same old behaviours which cause the same old problems. They often blame someone or something else, but from the outside it's pretty plain to see that if they were simply to change the way they do something, their situations and relationships would also change. For the better, I'm guessing. It's so easy to see this in others, especially when it impacts you in some way. It is harder to see these same patterns in ourselves, but we are all on the unwilling scale somewhere when it comes to change. This is why we need to be purposeful in our pursuit of change.

The primary reason people don't change is fear. I think most of us are ok with the idea of change, but we resist the fact that *we* need to change. Fear is the road block that shouts 'STOP!' to the parts of us that seek the path of change - because that would take us admitting that there are areas we can grow and improve in.

I have a theory that if we could remove the fear our lives would be dramatically changed - our workplaces, community groups, churches, marriages, friendships and relationships with our kids would be opened up to fresh possibility. If only fear didn't tell us to STOP!

I believe the most radical thing you could ever do is go on a pursuit of purposeful change.

You see most of us are standing at the 'STOP!' sign knowing something needs to shift whilst letting those big red letters of danger in front of us limit our forward movement. Whilst we are stood here at the road block we get frustrated, because we hate to be stuck, but the fear of the unknown keeps us here and so can't move forward. We live lives which are unfulfilled, like a shadow of the life we once hoped for. Pile on top the fear of admitting we need to change (which speaks to the insecurities we have about the desire to be seen as good or maybe even perfect) and we end up pointing fingers elsewhere when we hit these road blocks, trying to shift the blame for our life un-lived to other people or circumstances outside of our control. It takes a brave person to point a finger at them self; and it takes a brave person to be willing to climb over the road block onto the unknown path ahead.

In my work as a life coach, I help people negotiate the road blocks of fear and change. That change always begins within themselves; they are brave people who are radical enough to go on a pursuit of purposeful change. They invest their time, money and energy pointing the finger inwards towards themselves - not in blame, but in the name of change. You see why I love my job?!

Change is what keeps us growing; change is the sign you are still alive. Change is the greatest gift you can give yourself to keep you moving towards the life you really desire; closing the gap between the person you are and the person you hope you can be. Change is usually less about the external situations that we are disappointed with, than about the person we are that leaves us wanting to be more.

So, how do we become the brave souls who look inwards and start to negotiate our own road blocks with a view to moving forwards? How do we impact our relationships without blaming others and pointing fingers when we are hurt or let down? How do we create a culture of change within ourselves that impacts the world around us?

How does this change thing work? Good question.

The answer is fairly simple and strangely complicated at the same time. So, let's start with the easy bit. In order to change you need to know where you are and where you want to be. We will call where you are HERE, and where you want to be THERE. Change is the process of getting from HERE to THERE. Simple!

The tricky thing is that there are various hurdles along the way.

Firstly, there is the great big road block situated HERE on your journey that screams 'STOP!' It tells us that HERE is way better than THERE; it says 'Look at what you have HERE, this is fine! There are worse places to be than HERE'. The reason we listen to that voice is that it is laced with some truth. If the voice telling us to 'STOP!' straight-out lied to us, we would recognise the deception and throw it out like old rotten fruit. When the voice of fear is laced with truth we recognise the legitimacy in it and give that voice more airtime, wondering if there's more to this than we first thought.

The reality is that there are reasons you are HERE - there's a reason you have been camping out HERE for so long, other than the fear of what is ahead. HERE is providing something for you. The sadness is that so many people are change averse because of this truth-laced lie; they listen to it and forget it is not the full picture. The *whole* truth is that very often HERE is not at all better than THERE and we really, really shouldn't stay HERE a moment longer. Fear is a clever liar; it speaks to the part of us that craves safety and security and voices its concern in a way that forces us to freeze and not move forwards. It's important to know where HERE is and what HERE holds.

Secondly, we can get tripped up by not having any clue where THERE is and what it would be like to be THERE.

We know that our current reality isn't working, but we can't imagine THERE - and so we feel that we have no other option than to stay HERE. This is particularly tricky if your area of change involves other people. It is hard enough to change yourself, never mind leading others to change. If you are the person leading other people (friends, family, spouse or colleagues) through change, it is key that you offer them more than 'We can't stay HERE!' You need to offer them an alternative. People need the inspiration of 'what else?' in order to change, and that 'what else' needs to be a better option if we are going to leave what we know and journey somewhere new. The part of us which is risk and change averse, our humanity, needs to be inspired to something greater than what is currently available. We crave that inspiration; which is why knowing that HERE isn't working is often not enough incentive to promote change.

I bet right now you can identify a place where you currently are that is not the best for you. Throughout this book you will be given ways of identifying HEREs that are not your Eden; but you already know those - it may even be the reason you ended up with this book in your hands. HERE is no longer working for you, so staying HERE is driving you crazy.

We know where we are unhappy, stuck, unfulfilled. We know when our relationships let us down or trigger us to be our worst selves, not our best.

The problem is knowing how to get away from HERE. This is when you need a THERE: the thing that will inspire you and the people connected to you to keep moving forwards. This is why we need to dream and imagine and believe in the power and purpose of change - this is what will inspire us to move.

The third thing that can keep us stuck is that we don't know how to get from HERE to THERE. That path is an enigma, shrouded in mystery, and as I will explain later on, this kind of stuff is not binary or black and white; it's less like a road map and more like a conversation. For many people that is hard to hold - we love a road map and unless we can offer a point-by-point description of how we will move forwards, it's hard to get past the road block.

So our resistance to change is threefold:

1. We don't want to admit we need to change; that means admitting we are not perfect.
2. We can't find the better alternative - we don't know what else is possible.
3. We don't know how to get to something better - there isn't a road map of how to change.

Eden is a place we hold in our heart like a compass; something within us craves relationships healthy enough that we can thrive in them. Healthy relationships are the partnership between healthy people, and healthy people are those who welcome change. You cannot create your Eden if you cannot change. They say the definition of madness is doing the same thing over and over and expecting a different result. Too many people, and therefore too many relationships fall into this category of 'mad'. We do the same thing, be the same people, carry on as we have always done - and then act surprised when nothing changes. Madness! The only way out of this loop is change. You have to do something or be someone different if you want the outcome to be different.

It's time to stand at that road block; instead of feeling the fear and freezing, it's time to do something different and get a new outcome.

You are reading this for one of three reasons - either my mother bought you this (which is quite likely if you live East of the Atlantic), someone gave it to you (which means they may be trying to tell you something!) or the idea of finding Eden highlights that somewhere inside your heart you desire more, something different, something other to your current reality. It's time to take on some road blocks.

Some of the chapters in this book will help you realise where you are HERE at the road block and fear is keeping you stuck. Some of them will help you to dream about the THERE, to imagine what else could be possible in your world. Some of the chapters will help you to find some next steps as to how to move from HERE to THERE.

One of my greatest sadnesses is when I see bad habits or patterns of behaviour which have had a hold on me for years, if not decades. In the time I have been a nail biter, my whole skin has changed three times - that's 21 years. In the time I have been an emotional M&M's eater my skin has changed twice - over 14 years. It took me a whole skin change to see how I could support my son's growth in confidence better; how to hold space for my introverted husband, how to not get angry with work colleagues who triggered me. My history is that change often stops at skin level: but I don't want this to be my future. I would love for all of you to go on a journey of replenishment, regeneration and renewal. I would love for your heart, mind and soul to catch up and maybe even take over your external change process. I would love for your growth and purposeful change to be more than skin deep.

I realised when I was sat at my desk at work feeling alone in a crowd that something had to change. It wasn't something out there, it was something in me. I realised HERE wasn't working and although I had no idea what THERE looked like, I decided to go searching for it. I realised when I would rather spend time away from my husband than with him that something had to change. I realised I could keep pointing fingers at him or be willing to look at myself and be willing to change what was HERE in me. I realised when my daughter told me I was always on my laptop that something HERE had to change. I realised I could change my current HEREs all over my life and in all of my relationships if only the road block of fear didn't stop me any longer, if only I could dream big enough to be inspired to find 'what else', if only I was willing to start a journey into the unknown.

In the past five years I have changed more than in the two skin cycles before that. I thought that naming all my faults and flaws and the places I needed to change would make me miserable and ruin any scrap of self esteem I had, the opposite has been true. I am happier, more content, more confident and more fulfilled because I am creating something life giving in the weird wonky imperfect life that I have.

The journey to find something new can still be scary but I know that moving and changing is bringing me to life and that is now my inspiration to tie on my trainers and start running - to do something badly, then start to do something better with a hope to one day doing something beautiful.

CHAPTER 1:
WELCOME...
finding soul connection

Have you ever noticed that one of the the most powerful words we can ever utter to another human being is 'Welcome'?

We love to be told we're doing well, we love to be praised and valued and recognised but more than these things we desperately want to be welcomed. Welcome is the foundation deeper than praise or performance, it holds truer than recognition for what you do or what you achieve; being 'welcome' means being given permission to be yourself. When 'you're welcome' you get to fully show up, you get to take off the masks of 'okay' and 'coping', you can be celebrated and loved for who you truly are, and when 'you're welcome' you know there is a security that allows the less attractive bits that wriggle under the surface and refuse to stay hidden to come out and not negate the fact that you belong. We all want to feel like we are a part of something, that we are connected to others with a bond that is not easily broken. 'Welcome' is the green light to start building deep connection. When you know you're welcomed, then you know that you are tied to another human being with a bond of acceptance.

It's sad to say, but I expect that you have felt welcomed somewhere, but then you felt the pain when the tether was strained, maybe past its limits, to breaking point. I look back at my life and recognise the see-saw of acceptance and disappointment repeated over and over again. The truth is that I'm yet to find a human being who hasn't experienced this type of disappointment etched in their story somewhere. I'm yet to meet a person who hasn't been wounded because the space they thought they could trust to fully show up in, to be seen and then thrive in, wasn't safe enough. The places we thought were brimming with welcome became a breeding ground for wounding.

If you have ever been let down or disappointed, I encourage you to start a journey that will help you to lean in when it's easier to retreat, and show up when it's easier to hide. It may just be that you find something that will help you heal or help you move on. I hope that you will find some things to ponder, that will encourage you to hope, to see that you are in fact able to trust again, and that the disappointments you experienced in this less than perfect world are not the end of the story.

Human beings require deep soul connection in order to thrive.

This is the foundation that this entire book is built upon. I thought I'd let you know that upfront because this is important stuff. It might be that this idea stirs something up in you already; if so, I'd stop and camp out here for a moment.

Give yourself the space to let whatever is here, be here. So often we recognise disappointment and quickly move on pretending we didn't really see it, afraid to give it a voice in case we can't quieten it down again. It may be that the idea of deep soul connection touches a sore spot. It might be you feel like you've never quite found it, or that when you did somewhere down the line it disappointed you or left you empty. You may currently be in a relationship space that causes some sadness - maybe you're lonely, disconnected, hurting; maybe your kids are distant and you don't know how to reach them, your marriage is breaking apart, your friends have let you down; maybe your relationship status is not what you hoped it would be by this stage of life; maybe your school, faith community or work place is somewhere you feel isolated in. Maybe you've been hurt by a colleague, damaged by a parent, let down by a leader or manager. Whatever is here, that's okay - bring it all, it's all welcome here. I'd encourage you to be honest about where you're at, take off the masks; take stock for a moment. Maybe before we go any further it's worth considering where you are at right now. Look at the relational landscape around you and get your bearings when it comes to the idea of deep soul connection.

So pop the book down. Really - put it down. And just notice what is here for a while.

....

I did this about two and a half years ago. I didn't have this book to pop down but I did put my life down for a while (only four days, don't worry!)

I had realised that I was feeling permanently dissatisfied. I could feel lost and alone in a room full of people and the spaces which had felt so safe and welcoming now seemed confusing and unsure. On paper I had the perfect life, but the reality felt broken and empty. I knew my HERE was not where I wanted to be but I couldn't find any alternative.

I was invited by a friend to go on a retreat called The Destiny Project. It was a Christian coaching retreat around identity and as I hopped on a plane to Chicago, I had no idea what was ahead, I just sensed this was an important step to something new. At this point I had quit my job, left the roles I had served in for many years as a volunteer and I was struggling to step into church - the place I had found my strongest sense of home in for the ten years before that. I was weary in my parenting and struggling in a number of my friendships.

So I checked out of real life for four days and headed to this retreat.

I met my ride at the airport. About 20 minutes into the journey, I realised I had found a kindred spirit and I started to breathe again. By the end of the journey, this stranger had become a friend, the type of friend where you can say anything and know it's trusted. Something had started to shift...

We walked into a house full of over 20 women where I knew two people - one I had known a few months, one a few hours, yet somehow in that house in the middle of America surrounded by snow and not much else, I found home. It was in this house that I started to look inwards at the person I was becoming whilst having a crowd of beautiful witnesses cheer me on as I sought truth. We laughed and cried and deep friendships were made. It was here that I decided that blaming everything 'out there' was a stance that was keeping me stuck and that change had to start with me.

I hardly ever get to see these women, they live thousands of miles away in several different states, but they have my heart and I have theirs. What was modelled in those four days in snowy Chicago is what happens when you let down the barriers and welcome others into your journey. Not once over those four days was there negativity, gossip, comparison, exaggeration or competitiveness; instead there was witnessing, as we each walked baby steps on our own journeys.

In this house the usual rules didn't apply and it gave us all space to dream again. What I decided in those four days was that I didn't like the 'normal rules' where we live isolated lives, where we are afraid to show up, where we self-protect and hide away. I hated the normal rules of pretending to be perfect whilst tearing down those in front of us who seem to have made it. I decided that the home I had found with these girls who I barely knew was a home I wanted to build in the real world with my family and friends and co-workers. I wanted all of my people back home to feel and experience what it is like to be fully welcomed and find healing like I had.

That was two and a half years ago and my current reality is very different to the one I experienced back then. My life is different now because I decided to change it; actually, it is because I decided to change me. I am different and I my relationships are different. I now welcome myself, and I do all I can to welcome those around me to a place where they can be the best, most authentic, most deeply true version of themselves. I have stopped hiding; what you see is what you get. I don't pretend to be perfect, because quite frankly, I am a terrible actress. I ask for what I need and I dream about who I can become.

I have a job I love and a family I am building something sweet with. I am still tempted to self-protect and sometimes still do, but my recovery time is less and I don't dwell there like I once did. My life is not perfect, I and my relationships are still in progress; but I and they are now *on purpose*, they are heading somewhere rather than stagnating.

I am now in a place where I feel that tether of acceptance because the spaces I have co-created with others are healthy and honest.

I don't know what your current reality is, but I would love for you to experience that life-giving home space that I found in snowy Chicago. I would love for you to change up the rules a little.

I would love for you to experience healthy honest friendships and marriages and work places where you feel truly welcomed as you co-create something beautiful with the people in your world.

As you have thought about your current reality - the good, bad and the ugly, hear me when I give you all the permission you need to allow yourself to be welcomed enough here to fully show up, even if you don't yet have that permission anywhere else outside of these pages.

There are some questions on the next few pages which will help you to think about the idea of 'welcome' and 'home'. They will help you to find your dot on the map labelled 'YOU ARE HERE'. If you haven't journalled before, it's just a case of writing, drawing or doodling your thought patterns around an idea. Give it a go and remember that we are just putting on our running shoes - these are your first few steps on the path to discovery.

JOURNAL TIME

Where do you feel fully welcomed?
(which relationships, actual spaces, groups of people...)

JOURNAL TIME

Where are you feeling disappointed or disconnected?
How does this impact you?

JOURNAL TIME

What MUST you have in a relationship to be able to thrive?

CHAPTER 2:
INTRODUCING EDEN...
'home' as it was first intended

This book is about helping you to find, build and keep deep soul connection in all areas of your life. When you experience this, I believe you will discover that you are thriving, that you will experience aliveness and fulfilment and you will realise that you can maintain this even when seasons change and circumstances smash like waves on the rocks. I am convinced that deep soul connection is what keeps ships afloat and heads above water when storms hit and when the skies turn dark, and that these relationships will continue to be the foundation when things are bright, good and going well.

You see, there is something within each human being that is seeking and yearning for that perfect place of connection, a little piece of relational paradise in our world where nothing is broken or damaged, hurting or hard, where we can be un-shrouded by our shame, and unconditionally loved when our true self is revealed beneath the unravelled coverings of self-protection.

We are searching for a place where our souls feel at home.

Home is not just a physical place, it is the space where you experience all the safety you need to fully connect; home is the internal compass of the soul. There is a navigational tool inside us that is always pointing and leading us forwards to a place where we can be our truest self, where we can be loved and nurtured and where we can rest and dwell. Sadly, many homes are broken and that is often our reality; the very place we feel should be safest becomes dangerous and damaging; wounds from here cut deep. We aren't just searching for any old home, we are searching for a home we can thrive in. We are searching for a place we are welcome and wanted, settled and secure.

I wonder if what we are searching for is 'Eden'. Let me explain…

Eden was paradise. It was where human beings were placed in order to grow and develop together. Here, man and woman experienced deep soul connection; they were naked, their truest uncovered self; they were fully seen and fully loved. It was in Eden that they were connected with each other and with their Creator, the one who whispered the deep truth of who they were and what they were here for, as they wandered with him in the cool of the day. In Eden, human beings thrived when their true self was seen and celebrated, their purpose was revealed and they felt real fulfilment and connection. Eden was home - and home is the place where we get to be our most authentic self, it is our safe place where we get to simply be and not have to be masked or covered, or have to perform or keep up appearances.

It was not just in Eden where these needs are felt. We feel them too.

We were all created to search for Eden - this paradise of acceptance, purpose and presence. We feel the yearning for Eden most deeply when we instead experience the piercing disappointment of imperfect community, broken relationships and places that feel like hell instead of paradise.

We don't often get to live in paradise but the search to rebuild and reclaim it is a bubbling desire that continues in us all.

I wish I could hand you a road map that would lead you directly to Eden: a 'follow the dots' to a place of perfection, but that would be too easy, right? And if it's that easy it's probably not real. Instead let's explore what Eden provided and identify where Eden isn't at the moment. This exploration will draw you towards the discomfort you feel when that soul connection is not felt, where the places you thought would be safe have not been, where the perfect relationship has turned out to be more imperfect than you ever thought. We will go there, not because I want you to be unhappy, disappointed or unfulfilled but because when you know what isn't, then you can start to dream about what could be, you can begin the journey from HERE to THERE.

What marriage do you dream of? What friendship do you crave? What faith community or work place or small group do you wish you were a part of? What connection are you yearning for? Where is home not home? Because home is not just found in the bricks and mortar at the end of your address, it is found in the people we welcome in and who welcome us in - we find it through intimate relationship in family, friendship and community.

One of my early experiences of 'Eden' was at my teenage second home. I met Clare on day one at senior school, we were put in the same class fresh out of little school with oversized blazers and knee high socks. She was tall and confident and I was little and out of my depth - I suspect she was too but my 11 year old self found solace in the boldness she seems to wear over her blazer and knee socks. She lived with her mum and sister about 15 paces from the school gates and it quickly became tradition to go back to hers on a Friday after library duty via the chip shop.

Clare's house was one of the first places outside of the houses of my blood relatives where I found home. We ate chips and gravy and learned facts about New Kids on the Block, practiced dance moves and talked about boys and school. I rang my first crush from her phone and was picked up from a snivelling heap when it didn't end well.

Over the next seven years there would be more conversations about boys, lots more tears and even more laughter. I was playfully admonished by her mum for slouching on the sofa as she accepted me in a way that caused me to kick my shoes off and make myself at home in hers.

By the time we left for university I'd grown a foot and my legs hung over the edge of the sofa where I regularly slept. There was a 'me' shaped bottom print on my favourite chair by the window and I could get the shower to just the right temperature without even thinking about it.

Leaving this home to go to university was almost as hard as leaving the house I had grown up in.

Here was where I found friendship, love, laughter; here I had gone from a tiny 11 year old to a lankier 18 year old creating memories with tears and hugs and marmite on toast.

This house was not perfect but I had found a place I could belong, a home from home, my first taste of Eden.

Every now and again someone hands us a key to open the gates to experience Eden but the truth is that most of the time we have to be willing to create it within ourselves first, and then re-create it in our homes, families and other relationships. We are called to be home makers, to be builders of what we desire, and my hope is that you will pick up tools along the way that will help you to build and create something beautiful for your self and for those who are lucky and blessed enough to tiptoe into the home you are creating - whether literally or metaphorically. This book is a call to action that will ask you to yearn and dream, and then get into the gritty work of creating and building.

So roll your sleeves up - it's time to start the search for Eden.

CHAPTER 3:

AROUND THE EVENING FIRE...

there is no road map to Eden

Imagine with me a moment…

The night sky is clear, littered with diamond stars, the milky moon peeking from behind the gentlest whisper of a cloud. The air is mild, with a cool tinge that you can only feel at the edges of the day. The work is done for the day, there is a settling down, a quieting as the fervour of labour gives way to the peaceful pace of rest. This is the time when the fire is lit and one by one men and women gather to take their place sat under the expanse of indigo sky; this is when in long-ago times and far-away places the tribe members met to pass on wisdom and discuss ideas and new thoughts. It was here, as the fire and the mind were stoked, that embers lit up the creative source of imagination and beauty. Over countless centuries and across the width of the globe, elders would gather for wise counsel, to tell stories, to share images with deeper meaning and parables with many layers of learning, as the fire light danced across their wizened faces. It was here that laughter and heartache mingled with fresh thought and ancient wisdom. It was around the evening fire that both connection and counsel were found.

There is an invitation waiting for you to gather around the evening fire with us; take your place here.

Let go of the burdens of the day, put down your work tools whatever they may be. Relinquish toil and fervour for a while; you have been working hard, but this is not the space for work, this is a time to be. Around this fire you get to dream about the world you want to live in, you get to imagine what might be possible for the relationships in your world. It is here that you will hear new ideas, pass on practiced wisdom, and it is here that you will find rest.

Let this book be an invitation to gather around the evening fire rather than a road map to reach a destination where stories, ideas and tools are offered. This book is flickers of orange and firelight-red rather than black and white answers. Notice that there is space for you under the stars in the sky, to sit with this tribe and their night time stories, close to the fire, feeling the warmth of new ideas and shared hearts. Let yourself explore how to build something new, how to apply the ancient wisdom of a garden paradise known as Eden, the home defined by deep soul connection, to the world you live in.

So often we seek a how-to guide. We desire the simplicity of a+b=c; a point by point list of instructions to put together the perfect flat-packed relationship. But we also know that there is something deeper needed that will require more of us, if we are to experience spaces that hold the heart of Eden, the essence of home.

Relationships are not logical equations of right and wrong, and intimacy is not binary black and white. Authentic connection requires you to colour outside the lines.

Your soul searches for Eden because this is where man was placed to thrive, but there is no cosmic blueprint we can all photocopy and take home to follow. What there is though, is the fireplace. This is a journey of pondering and dreaming; it is about trying to create something new and different as you journey into unknown territory. Here you will get a place to think and some hands to hold as you build a home that is real enough, safe enough, brave enough and bold enough to offer yourself and others in your world a place to thrive.

Look around you. You are not alone.

You are not the only one who searches. Your path may feel lonely at times, you are treading new ground, but you are not alone on your quest. We each carry this desire to thrive. We all look for a welcome sign to show up. We wait for the key of permission to be handed to us so that we can open a door and be invited in to a place tender enough to know and be known.

We sit with you and smile across the flickering flames, we know you can do this, we believe it possible because we know it was always intended. Heaven on earth is not a new idea; there is a sacred invitation to usher in Eden to a broken world that craves acceptance and life-giving relationship. The elders have seen it happen, the lines etched on their faces testify to years of exploration and creation; look deep in their eyes and see a knowing. They have walked many others through this process, they have seen the dream become a reality, they have seen that life happens when breath and dirt mingle and new life is ushered in where once there was only dust.

This book will act as your tribe as you journey and journal towards new relational ground. Of course, you are unlikely to be physically alone on this journey once you step out of the metaphors in this book - we are creating something new with what we have, where we are. You have friendships and jobs, marriages and kids - we are not about to scrap your old life to create a perfect new one… that is not the journey. You will be picking up and practicing tools within the book to then take outside of these pages to search and create healthy 'homes' with the people who are already stood with you in your life. So as we step out of the metaphor of the tribe space that this book offers us let's just pause and identify what our relational landscape currently looks like.

I'd like to offer you a tool I often use in my work as a life coach. This tool is called a wheel of life and is designed to help you take a wide view of your life.

It breaks your world down into small chunks, facilitating the path to initiate and implement new ideas without becoming overwhelmed by the feeling that we need to change our whole world all at once. The wheel is often broken down into different areas of your life like health, work and finances but we are going to use this tool to identify different relational spaces you have in your life.

These are the different 'homes' you live in - the places you dwell in day-to-day. These are the 'homes' you are going to be investing in and trying out your new tools in - these are the places you are searching for the welcome of 'Eden' in.

In each of the eight blank pie pieces I would like you to identify a different relationship (either individual or group) which is important in your world. You will use this wheel to help you throughout this book so make sure you fill it in now.

I have done mine below to give you an example, then there is a blank wheel for you to fill in. I encourage you to have family of origin (your parents/siblings etc) in there, as well as your children and spouse or significant other if you have them. The rest is up to you - there are examples below but this is by no means an exhaustive list.

Your family of origin
Your spouse/partner/significant other
Your child or children
Your boss
Your church or place of worship
A colleague or group of workmates
Your small group
An ex-partner if significant
Your close friends - individuals or groups

MY RELATIONAL WHEEL:
THE 'HOMES' I DWELL IN DAY TO DAY

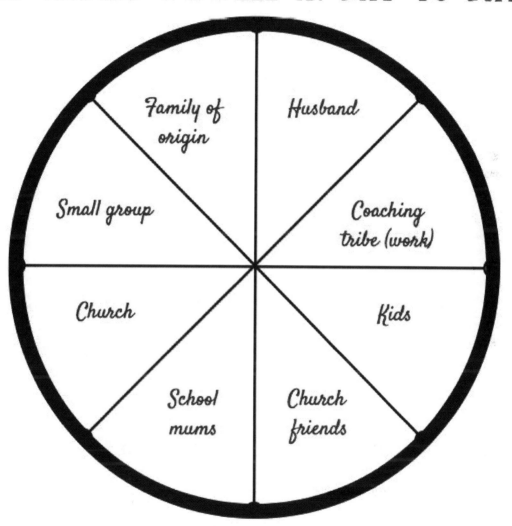

YOUR RELATIONAL WHEEL:
THE 'HOMES' YOU DWELL IN DAY TO DAY

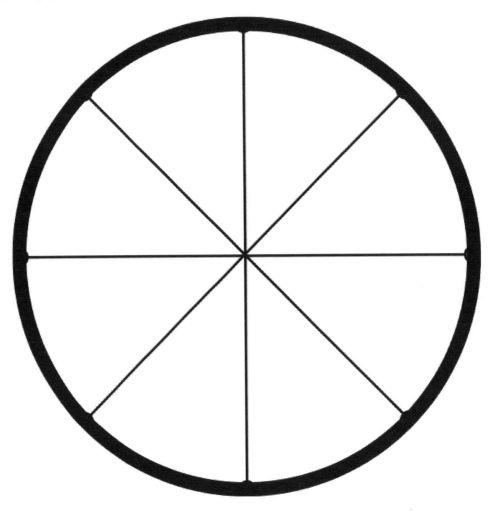

CHAPTER 4:
TELL US YOUR STORY...
of what 'home' has been for you

Before we explore what could be, it's important to know what is and what has been. So first, I invite you to tell us your story - this place is safe enough. Maybe you have a broken home, maybe your have lost your tribe. Maybe you are starting to build something beautiful, honest and true but have run out of tools. Maybe you have never been allowed to dream the dream. Your story is welcome here whatever it looks like.

Your story is your gift to the world, with its highs and lows, its ups and downs, a narrative of grace. Sometimes the villain's voice has gotten too loud and you have found yourself doubting the impact and worth of your story. Maybe you are so focused on certain characters or certain chapters that you haven't allowed yourself to remember the whole story you have walked so far - the beauty of the tensions, the triumphs and the battles. Let your story sing out its sacred song and inspire us with melodies of hope and inspiration. Remember what you had momentarily forgotten about the person you were and the person you dreamed of becoming. Ponder the twists and turns and consider the myriad of characters that have made up your epic tale from birth to now. Notice the threads that have woven through each chapter, plot lines you hadn't noticed before and sentences that mean more now than ever before.

Here is a place where your voice can be heard, the fire is lit and it's time to tell your story; the unique narrative of who you are and where you have come from.

Use the space over the page in any way that is helpful for you (be as creative as you wish!). Write, draw or create in another way - whatever helps your story unfold.

You are going to plot your story chapter by chapter. The questions below will help you to focus on a season starting with your early memories. Once you have jotted down your responses you are going to go back and add a title to this chapter. Try to boil down all you have noted down into a phrase that captures the essence of that season, a thread that is woven throughout.

As an example, my first chapter covers from my earliest memory aged about 5 until I was 11 years old and is entitled 'The Golden Years'. It tells the story of a girl who was full of life and energy who ran around with her brothers, had many friends and felt no need to filter herself for the sake of others. She laughed loud and played bold, she remembers long summer days of grubby knees and sugar-sticky fingers, of cartwheels and stitches from falling in cricket matches.

A later chapter would be called 'Finding me' - it is the season of about four years in my late 20s where I questioned everything I was. I moved jobs, changed friendship groups and queried aspects of my faith and beliefs. It was a season that was hard and rough where the air seemed a little thinner and harder to breathe in. My marriage was stretched, we had a baby and a toddler and hadn't slept a full night in half a decade. I had no clue who I really was or where I was going. The chapter would be coloured with a darker palette, heavier tones.

Allow each chapter to form naturally and have as many as seems right for the life you have lived. There is a lot of journalling space; you don't need to fill it and you may need to add reams extra - whatever is fine! I will say, it is rare that we get to tell our whole story anywhere so give yourself the time to do your story justice.

Think back.
What do you remember?
What was true in your early years about the spaces you experienced at home - with parents, siblings and wider family, at school, church, with friends?
What was true of you?
What did you love?
What saddened you?
What were the milestones - the highs and lows?
What was your energy or the energy of this period of time?
What do you want the name of this chapter to be?

Now move onto the next chapter - go back to the questions above. Add in work places, new relationships, whatever unfolded in each stage, and keep on going until you reach the present day.

JOURNAL TIME

My Story...

JOURNAL TIME

My Story...

JOURNAL TIME

My Story...

JOURNAL TIME

My Story...

JOURNAL TIME

My Story...

CHAPTER 5:
LET THE
RENOVATION BEGIN...
dream the dream

About 18 months ago we began a building project on our home. I realised on day two that the glamour of TV home make-overs is not reality. Renovation is noisy, dirty, expensive work. Allowing walls to be torn down and new foundations to be built is no easy task - it takes grit and a whole lot of disruption. Our builder was amazing - a kind, thoughtful guy who genuinely acted in our best interests - I guess he knows from years of experience that very quickly the reality of renovation hits a client and the home itself like a wrecking ball.

The dreaming-up process was much nicer - colour palettes and fabric swatches; stone and wood and textures and furnishings. The dreaming stage is all about imagination and possibility, the concepts and the wonder. And then someone knocks a hole in your kitchen wall and the reality kicks in.

I sense that the dreaming stage is a vital one. Being able to hold in your mind's eye what you are working towards is the thing that keeps you going when the rain pours in the voids in the brickwork, and the only evidence you see of 'progress' is bigger and bigger holes in the ground. It is so important to us that we allow ourselves to dream. I have bumped up against people who cannot value the dreaming stage and cannot see the worth in allowing yourself the gift of wonder… they frown at the frivolity of it; they scorn the sense of delight found in imagining the very best. I sense these people may have dared to dream and then had to harness the disappointment of demolished dreams. I get that, we've all been there, right? I think the wisdom of dreaming is holding the vision out in front of you whilst not letting it direct your path so strongly that you miss the joy of wandering and wondering. What you discover when you allow the process to unfold is that the dream morphs like lava in a lamp, bubbling out into new and different shapes. It looks sort of similar but there is a fluidity to dreams that is beautiful if they are not held so tightly in the palm of your hand that you squeeze the life out of them.

For now, you get to dream. Imagine the textures and the shapes of the 'homes' you desire - remember the wheel with the pie pieces? These are the 'homes' we are going to dream about. Imagine what your marriage could feel like at its best. Imagine the scents of deeply connected friendships. Dream up the design of the parent you wish you could be for your kids. See these relationships at their very best, dream the dream and then dream some more. Focus on the details enough so that when you close your eyes it is close enough to touch and taste. Don't frown at the frivolity of dreaming.

New homes are not built overnight, and soon enough you need to decide if the dream is inspiring enough to start kicking holes in your walls. So dream big, dream well, dream boldly.

I am not an expert at home renovation but let me tell you what I have learned. Creating the dream space will cost more than you think. A lot more. Much of the cost goes on the bit underground that most people will never see - a good strong foundation. It has to get messy before it gets sorted and somewhere in the middle you may well find yourself crying into a mug of coffee because you can't see how this will ever get finished. Literally.

The problem with most people's dreams is that they are pipe dreams. Pipe dreams imagine that you are married to the Milk Tray man (or woman), have perfect children who never do anything wrong and friends who know exactly what to say when. Your boss would be perfect, your family of origin totally functional - Hollywood eat your heart out!

This is not about pipe dreams that can only be found by checking-out from reality, it is about allowing your heart to tell you the truth about the person you desire to become and how best you can show up for the people in your world. You cannot change another person; swapping husbands, friendship groups, churches, jobs or anything else is not going to change the only thing you have control over - yourself. What if you let yourself dream about what you can create when you are being your best self? What if you let go of the lie that you can only be content if everyone just deals with themselves and stops being so damn weird and dysfunctional to you? What if we each realised that instead of trading in Average Joe for Prince Charming we get to influence and impact Joe to inspire him to want to grow and develop and be the very best Joe he could be? When you are at your best, you will inspire the people around you to be their best too. And two bests make a right.

Now, hear me on this. There are times when you need to know that a relationship is not doing you any good AT ALL. If you are at risk, living the dream may mean moving away, drawing clear boundaries and letting yourself thrive in a redefined space. For many of us, it's less about moving home and much more about renovation.

Stay with the picture for a moment longer… you can only work on *your* house. It would be a touch inappropriate to pop round to your neighbour's and knock down walls because you can see how much better their home would be with a few tweaks. Sadly, we live in a society that sees our neighbour's need for renovation much more than the work we need to do on our own home. It's easier to point the finger than take responsibility for the work of our own hands.

As we continue this journey, let's stay close to home. This is not about all the dysfunctional things you see everywhere else, but about calling you to build the very best home you can and maybe in the process inspire others to do the work on their own homes.

Renovation begins with plans. The work begins with dreaming about what could be. So what do you dream of? What do you desire?

I'd like you to create a plan for the 'home' you desire. I get that for some of you the future seems out of your hands - you can't just magic up the guy or girl of your dreams, you can't choose your boss, you can't swap your parents. Pipe dreams look externally and they will only leave you looking at the lack. We are going to dream about something that is in your hands, that will leave you feeling inspired not stuck.

When we began our home renovation we knew that we wanted to have a kitchen where the whole family could dwell, and where there was room for anyone else who wanted to be there to come and dwell also. We wanted to create a spacious place that was the heart of our home. We knew that in order to do that we had to take down a wall, but when we were in the dreaming space we didn't know about planning rules, and heights of beams, we knew nothing about depths of foundations and measures between our house and the neighbours (that's a whole other story). The dream was to have a space big enough for a giant table that would be in the centre of the room, to have a seating area where people could gather, and to have giant doors to open the room to the outside. That was the dream. Open, spacious, full of people, gathered around the table. This was the inspiration for us to know that the dream was worth enough to bash walls down and to invite in a season of discomfort.

I'd like you to dream. Okay - I get this is tricky so I'll go first. I'm going to start dreaming out my pie piece labelled 'kids'. I have two children: a boy aged 9 and a girl of 8. This is my dream about the space I want to create in my family in order that I find my Eden with my kids.

I want to create a space where my children know they are deeply loved and accepted for who they really are - loved in thought, word and deed. I desire to know exactly how to show them love and to provide them with tangible examples that regularly show how much I love them. I want to be a parent who helps my children to thrive by them knowing appropriate boundaries but having a spirit of adventure and playfulness too. I want to shout less and play more. I dream of teenagers who want to come and talk to me about their world so I am setting that foundation in place now by intentionally inviting their conversations in, even when I am busy. In my job, I can choose not to work between 3.30pm and 8.00pm when they are home from school, so the dream is to close the laptop, ignore the pings on my phone and play board games, paint pictures, kick balls and have coffee dates with them. I dream of having a thriving relationship with my kids which is known for our affection rather than confrontation, for sharing rather than separation.

You'll notice that the dream is about what *I* can create, who *I* can be. The dream is within my reach, so it won't paralyse me into inaction. I am not bashing holes in anyone else's house - I could have dreamed a dream based on who I want my kids to be, or the change in behaviour I want to see in them (and believe me - there are several I could have picked from!) but that only causes me to see the disappointment of what isn't rather than the possibility of what could be.

So now it's your turn. Choose one relationship to start with and then build on it as you go along.

Go back to your wheel of relationships and choose a pie piece.
What is your dream about this 'home' you wish to create?
What words and pictures would be important in this space you want to create?
What will give you the inspiration to start the renovation?
What values do you want to honour in this 'home'?

Play with some ideas; and remember that ideas sometimes take time to finalise. Create in any way that helps you to dream well - it may be with words, pictures, images… but use the questions above to let yourself dream and be inspired enough to let yourself kick down the walls. Some of you will jot down a list of words, others of you will want to 'colour outside the lines'.

We will come back to some of these ideas so I encourage you to make the time to play around with some thoughts.

JOURNAL TIME

My Home Renovation Dream...

JOURNAL TIME

My Home Renovation Dream...

JOURNAL TIME

My Home Renovation Dream...

CHAPTER 6:

BEAUTIFUL...

seeking beauty over perfection

Let's go back to the roots of Eden, the story of creation found in the Christian bible. This is the place where the Divine Creator dreamt up a place which would be called 'home' for his most breathtaking creation. This creation was an image-bearer of his divinity, crafted in his likeness, with aspects of his heart and his spirit. The home he created for them was perfect for them. He knew what they needed to thrive and he provided it for them because he loved them. He created light and dark, oceans and mountains, plants and animals, food and fruit; and then the pinnacle of his creative expression was 'man'.

Some believe the story to be gospel truth, others believe it to be an allegory, a poem; others hold it with some scepticism… Whatever your belief, an exploration of the heart behind Eden is helpful for us in defining what we are building here together.

So Adam and Eve are the main characters in the story of Eden.

The original texts that tell the Eden story are written in Hebrew, and when we look back at what was first written thousands of years ago we see that Adam and Eve are incredibly significant to us many, many years later. In Hebrew, Adam actually means 'mankind' or 'human' and Eve is translated as 'life' or 'living'. These names are not random and this is not the story of two people who bear no connection to us. These names are intentional, this is the story of 'mankind', of the 'living' ones - not just the first ones, but all the ones who came after.

Adam and Eve are the main characters in the story of Eden, but so are we.

The dream was for man to thrive and experience deep connection.
The Creator created so that man could prosper, multiply, get bigger, go deeper: *thriving*.
He created a space where he could be with them and they could be together: *connection*.

Thriving and connection.

They seem to be intrinsically linked and divinely valued in this story of mankind, and we can sense the same importance of these two things some thousands or millions of years later. Eden is the setting for the story of the living ones who are truly living.

What does that mean for us today?

Think of someone you know who you are inspired by, someone who you look up to. Is the reason you look up to them because they are the richest person in the world? Maybe, but for most of you I doubt it. Is it because they are the most highly educated person on the planet? Maybe, but probably not. Are they the person you would want to offer you wisdom? I'm guessing yes. Are they thriving as a person? Probably. Would they be the person you would want advice from on your relationships? Again, I suspect yes. My guess would be that the things you're inspired by in this person are the things we all desire in life - they may not, however, be the things we initially think we need in order to thrive.

Although our Western culture promotes prosperity, power and prestige, our souls seek out the wise ones who are *thriving* and who model good *connection*.

Final question... is the person you admire perfect? No, they are not, I'm sure.

Thriving and connection are the cries of our soul whilst perfection is the persistence of our culture.

When you think of Eden, the place created for thriving and connection, I suspect the first thing you think of in this paradise is perfection. We imagine that Eden was perfect in every way - the surroundings were untainted by global warming and pollution; the relationships were untainted by wrong choice or bad intention. Before someone picked a bad apple - man, woman and the Divine lived in perfect harmony - right? When we think of Eden, we imagine perfection.

When we see that we are in a place which is imperfect, we have a tendency to focus on what is 'not right'. We blame the gaps and the 'nots', we point fingers at the wrongs and the blemishes. If only the imperfections weren't here in me, in those I live with, work with, do life with - then it would be perfect and I would thrive! We think back to Eden and see the perfection of paradise and it highlights the faults in our own worlds. We see the sickness, the wrong doing, the bad intentions and evil outcomes; on a more personal scale we see the selfishness, the meanness, the lack of kindness in our relationships with others - we see the imperfect. We compare our imperfect homes to an image of the perfect Eden and fall head first into discontentment.

We compare our imperfect relationships within our family, workplaces, churches and friendships. We look around us and see ample evidence of people thriving and connection being made - we see it and we yearn for it.

The strange truth of course is that these things you are comparing to are not perfect either. The strange truth is that imperfect people thrive and imperfect people experience deep connection. It is not their perfection that creates their Eden, and it is not the imperfections in you or those around you which stop you from finding yours.

The truth is not so black and white - the truth is that when God created, he never once declared anything 'perfect', He never once said that we or the world was flawless or faultless: this is a misrepresentation of what the story of Eden tells us. When the Divine Breath breathed into his most precious creation and it came to life - he never pronounced it perfect, he declared it *beautiful*. The word he uttered in response to what he saw is often translated as 'good' but the more authentic meaning speaks to something which is 'beautiful to the senses'. The bar to measure by, even in Eden, was beauty not perfection. Sadly, we measure ourselves and the people in our worlds next to an unachievable bar.

It is a lie that perfect people are possible, and it is a lie that is tearing this creation apart. It is a lie that there is the perfect job, spouse, kids, parents... fill in the gap... You won't find it and you'll miss out on life looking for it.

The part of the Christian creation story that many people outside of the Christian faith wrestle with is that God made man then expected him to be perfect - to follow a list of rights and wrongs and do's and don'ts in order to be the perfect creatures placed in Eden. But when you were created and Divine Breath breathed into you, you were declared beautiful, not perfect.

We see our imperfections and we declare them ugly instead of seeing the beauty we hold.

The truth is that we seek perfection in our work places, marriages, friendships and families. What if instead of seeking perfect we instead became seekers of beauty within these relationships? Instead of black and white, what if we decided instead to see the myriad of colour? What if the opposite end of the spectrum from 'perfect' is not 'imperfect' but 'beauty'?

The people you admire and aspire to learn from are beautiful, not perfect; and somewhere down the line they started to believe the truth that beauty and perfection are very different things and started to live that truth out in their world. People who search for perfection only see the imperfect in more detail, people who search for beautiful start to notice the colour and the song in the lives that they already have.

If you think of Eden as being the picture of the place in which you can thrive, and the lens you look through is one called 'perfect', your journey and destination will be entirely other than if you look through the lens of 'beauty'.

When you consider the people and organisations in your world and aim for perfection it will be a different path than seeking beauty.

Eden is not a place of perfection but a place of beauty - this is what makes it paradise. What we should be seeking to build are places of beauty not perfection. When something is beautiful it can be seen in its entirely and appreciated for what it is, with different hues and textures. When something is perfect it has a long way to fall and can only keep its podium by being flawless, spotless, faultless. When something is beautiful the flaws don't change its beauty, the blemishes don't detract from the whole. When something is perfect and a flaw or fault is found, it tumbles and smashes under the weight of judgement. Something cannot be faultless and faulty at the the same time and where there is fault through the lens of perfection, there is blame.

It's so easy to see the blemishes in ourselves and others, the dark spots that shout out that we and they are not all that we should be. We then blame the blemishes for our lack of connection and our dissatisfaction in our homes, work places, churches and community groups on other people's flaws. The faulty is at fault.

Have you ever stood by a tall stained glass window, looking upwards as the sun streams through throwing colour and beauty as its shadow?

Brokenness does not mean something is not beautiful. When light is allowed to shine through, the faults and flaws can make something even more beautiful and breathtaking.

What if we stopped looking at other people's imperfections and our own short comings as being the things which hinder thriving and connection? What if your happiness at work was not so connected to your boss's broken attitude? What if your spouse's disconnection from you did not define your contentment as a person? What if your friendships with people had no measure of perfect or imperfect but of beauty instead?

It's a choice to look through a different lens - but you'd be amazed what you can see when you do. When you stop trying to recreate perfection you put down a large burden and your hands are free to build something else, to pick up shards of beauty that you had never noticed before. When you take your eye off the bar of perfection, you start to see the beauty.

Have you ever been frustrated because someone repeatedly focuses on what you can't do instead of what you can?

You probably know what it's like to feel like someone made a decision about you based on one or two incidents (that were probably not your finest hour) but you can't seem to shake the label they have given you however much you try. When they notice the un-mopped floor over the polished surfaces? When they see the late hours not the hard work? When they fix their eyes on the harsh word not the kind actions that surround it? It's hard when someone only seems to see your darkness and not your light - but I suspect we are capable of doing it to others just as much as it's done to us. We are quick to label people by the thing they did that hurt us, we find the lowest common denominator and let it define the whole person or relationship - and we ignore any of the beauty that is present. We love to label people as heroes or villains - we flip back to black and white.

Think back to the person you admire. Let me tell you right now - they are not perfect and you would find their imperfections if you spent enough time with them. Don't put them on the perfection pedestal; it's a long way to fall and they probably never asked to be put there anyway. What you see in them is the way they allow the light to shine through the stained glass window of their life; this is the beauty you can see. This beauty is about taking the broken pieces and choosing to put them together to make something beautiful. This beauty has been created by a wise soul who didn't sweep the broken glass under the rug so you didn't notice something got broken - they picked up the shards piece by piece and built something breathtaking with what they had.

Those who we see are thriving chose beauty over perfection. What if you decided to choose the same?

Let's pause for a moment and look at some of the glistening glass you see around you... let's take a moment to see what is here once we have thrown away the lens of perfection. Take some time to work through the questions below and allow yourself to not only notice what's here but as you pick it up and turn it over between finger and thumb, see that when it is brought into the light, it can become something quite beautiful.

In a moment I am going to ask you to start to notice the beauty that is already in your world by going back to the wheel of relationships you filled in earlier and choosing three pie pieces to focus on.

When seeking beauty over perfection, the reality is that we have to sometimes take intentional time to see something different if we are used to seeing what is broken.

It is a choice to put on your running shoes and head in a new direction. This exercise will help you to start noticing the beauty that is already in your world, it will help you to redefine your relationships and take them out of the good/bad/right/wrong/perfect/imperfect boxes. The problem with these boxes is that they end up creating heroes and villains - heroes on pedestals of perfection, designed to fall off when they disappoint or let down; and villains whose colour and beauty is not permitted because of the way they have hurt or impacted us for the negative. This way is messier for sure, but no person is all bad or all good; we are all a stained glass work in process.

You are going to pick three of the pie pieces or relational 'homes' from the relational wheel and then you are going to start to list the beauty you see in that person or space. I know that this may be hard if you are in a really tough season in one of these relationships but it can be seriously powerful to choose to see the beauty in someone in those painful hard times. It starts to break down the hero/villain titles and bust open those boxes that keep us stuck and restricted.

So grab a pen, choose your first person or relational space and simply start to list the beauty in them... they provide for our children, they choose to help others, they offer kind words, polished surfaces or hard work.

Feel free to keep going back to this to add things to your list as you notice something else and something else - once you start to seek beauty you'll be amazed what you can see.

One day you may even decide to share your list with the person you wrote it about. Truth sets us free, and there is something powerful in knowing the truth that we are valued by someone enough that they would intentionally seek the beauty in us. I'll leave that with you.

JOURNAL TIME

The beauty I see in............................

JOURNAL TIME

The beauty I see in..........................

JOURNAL TIME

The beauty I see in...........................

Now it's time to look inwards rather than outwards. When was the last time you looked at the beauty in yourself rather than the flaws? For some people this may be a much harder exercise than looking for beauty in others but I am going to encourage you to spend some time looking at yourself. It may help you to ask a few people that you love and trust to tell you the beauty they see in you, as a springboard if you don't know where to start. I urge you to do this at the start of the process and then keep adding to your list. My desire for you would be that you discover more and more of the beauty you offer the world as we journey together.

JOURNAL TIME

The beauty I see in myself...

CHAPTER 7:
PIONEER...
finding new ground where you are

I have to lean into my imagination when it comes to Eden, into living the dream as it was always intended because we can't jump on a bus and go there on a field-trip I'm afraid. Somewhere deep inside of each of us the hope of Eden still exists and this is why we all yearn to have it present in our world.

When I imagine what was true in Eden, I imagine man, woman and God walking in the garden after a day's work. I imagine that Eden was no walled English garden but an expanse of wild flora, an uncharted land teeming with things to discover. I imagine that there was much to see, much to learn, so much newness of life.

I imagine that life there was one of discovery and adventure. I imagine them wandering, finding, seeing new things, exploring new parts of the garden they had never seen before. I imagine new flowers and new creatures, untried pathways waiting to be found and experienced.

I believe that Eden was the home of the first pioneers. Just think, the land was new and beautiful - a gift from the cosmic Creator to his beloved. He had declared that it was good. When man was placed in the garden to thrive, he was given the space to explore, to name the new things he discovered and then claim them in all their beauty.

A pioneer is someone who is willing to be the first person to do something or go somewhere. Eden was new, it had not been charted out yet, it needed a pioneer to open up this new home and for it to be experienced in its entirety.

Part of thriving is being willing to discover what is new, to tread new ground, to explore what has not yet been found and to name it and claim it. The pioneer spirit lives within each of us but for many, the fear of the unknown keeps us stuck in the safety of what is comfortable. Especially in relationships and organisations, the status quo keeps us in the mundane, the ordinary, the unfulfilling and the uninspiring.

There is so much new ground in every existing relationship, organisation and family structure that goes unexplored because we are scared to be pioneers, scared of what is untamed and unknown. We don't explore something new and so we either cope with the old or give up and move to a whole new world altogether.

Several years ago I found myself in a relationship with my husband that felt stuck and unfulfilling. It was partly circumstantial - we had two young children and were both working a lot. We were tired and busy - and kind of grumpy too! We had been married about seven years and the itch was beginning to settle in.

We were not communicating with each other well and we were living from a place of scarcity when it came to the resources of time, energy and space. What we needed from each other, we didn't know how to provide well; we were a not-fun introvert/extrovert mix, and we were each becoming more and more unhappy within our marriage.

One day, prompted by something small enough that I can't even remember, it all came to a head. It was make-or-break time. Luckily, a good friend recommended a good marriage counsellor and she started us on a journey of finding new ground in our relationship. To start with it was hard to see that anything good could come from this relationship, but week by week we started to take baby steps into something new - a new way of communicating, a new way of disagreeing, a new way of loving better, a new way of explaining how we felt and what we needed.

Moving from what is currently here to something new is so much easier when you know where you're going - and sometimes we are given the gift of a destination to aim for. Sometimes, however, we have to be willing to take pioneer steps - we need to move from the currently predictable mediocre, with no definition of what the destination may look like. All we are offered is the open road and that inner compass that always points to home.

I think the hardest thing about a being a pioneer must be the moment you realise that you are going to have to leave the safe place you are in. As humans, we have a deeply planted DNA strand that tells us to stay put. That may not be scientific, but I know it's true. It's why we wallow in bad marriages, stay in jobs we hate, keep going out with friends who do us no good. Sometimes that DNA strand that tells us to stay stuck has a loud and powerful voice. It's there to protect us from harm, to keep us safe - I understand that…but sometimes safety is not fulfilling and protection keeps us isolated.

We have the 'stay still' DNA but we also have the 'pioneer' DNA, the desire to explore and find something new, the dream of the adventure and the desire to know what is outside of our borders. I guess the question is which one has the louder voice in your world? And is it time to turn the volume down on one to hear what the other has to say?

What if that relationship you feel stuck in held so much more? What if there were acres of undiscovered Eden that would bring you the most amazing amount of fulfilment if only you stepped one foot outside of your comfort zone? What if staying still is keeping you disconnected or isolated?

My husband and I have found a depth to our relationship that I never knew was there, but we had to be willing to say 'This is not enough, let's go and pioneer something new'.

There was a risk in this. We may have gotten lost along the way or been met by a beast we didn't know what to do with, but the voice telling us to try something new became louder than the voice that caused us to stay still. Very often we wait until the pain of staying where we are is so great that moving is the only option we have left. Too often pain is our only catalyst for change. When you are a pioneer your inspiration for change is not pain but curiosity.

The journey of the pioneer is being willing to step out from the comfort of what they know, all the good and bad. They trade this in for the new path, the call for adventure, the desire to discover what has not yet been found. Pioneers are curious creatures. They are willing to carve a way into unknown territory through thorns and thistles, not allowing the wide well-trodden path to entice them from their quest to take new ground.

Pioneers are also brave creatures. They are not brave because they are not afraid, they are brave because they go despite their fear. Pioneers embody the bravery that chooses to walk a new path that scares the pants off them because the drive to discover is stronger than the drive to stay stuck. Courage is not the absence of fear, right?! Courage is the willingness to step on new ground and to allow the possibility of what might *be* to outweigh the safety of what *is*.

Many of us have outgrown the homes we are dwelling in. Maybe the unwritten rules here are stifling, maybe the family dynamic here has become more and more dysfunctional and less and less fulfilling. Sometimes we end up living by rules we don't agree with just to keep the status quo, we play a role in order to not rock the boat, we silence and shrink to stop the ship from sinking.

Despite these things squeezing us into smaller versions of our true selves, it's tough to leave what is known and comfortable - even if it is a bit dysfunctional. Better the devil you know I guess? You know how to play by these rules, even if you don't like them. In this place everyone knows what is and isn't acceptable, what you are permitted to do or not, you know which mug to drink out of, which ornaments not to touch and which is Granny's chair that you are quite simply not allowed to sit in it even if you want to!

When you're in a place that dishonours your values, the dream of what could be diminishes as we find ourself thinking 'This can never change!' It may be you've tried to change it over the years, you moved an ornament or sat in 'the' chair - or maybe you subtly suggested that the rules could change in order to create a healthier space where you felt more accepted or welcomed... If these suggestions not taken well it definitely seems easier to stay put and keep quiet.

These things show up in a host of different ways and it takes a brave pioneer to carve out a new path and to find new territory.

I recognised in my marriage that I had hung a sign over the door that had been over me in other areas of my life for a long time. I have been on a journey recently of learning to express my needs well. Some time ago, someone said I was 'needy' and it seemed that 'needy' was bad. The unwritten rules of the house were that we don't tolerate neediness, it is annoying and a sign of weakness, and I took this into my marriage. Somewhere along the journey I just made an internal agreement that this must be right, because more than one time I spoke up with a need it got frowned at or scoffed at. I decided that being in the house labelled 'NO NEEDY PEOPLE ALLOWED' was okay, and that I could swallow down my needs in order to be acceptable, to fit.

Deep down I knew this wasn't the thing I wanted, but avoiding all the unwritten rules around being needy seemed a small enough price to pay to be allowed into the home. The 'stay stuck' DNA had the loudest voice. The thing was, it wasn't just the DNA voice that said needy was bad, other voices joined in and confirmed it. I can remember the discomfort in the work place when I cried because I got emotional about something I was passionate about. I remember the friend who looked with shock and surprise when I expressed a need from her. The Helen who was strong, together and helpful was fully acceptable, but when Helen was brave enough to show a deeper more emotional part of herself it provoked shock, discomfort and annoyance.

Then six months ago I went on a retreat and on the second day someone asked me why I always swallowed down my emotions instead of expressing what I needed. In this house there was no sign over the door reading 'NO NEEDY PEOPLE ALLOWED'. In this house the sign seemed to say 'ALL OF YOU IS WELCOME'. Over the next few days I struggled with an internal battle of what was right and wrong, good and bad. The black and white swirled like watercolours so that I couldn't distinguish between the two anymore, and at some point on that journey I realised that the internal voice that wanted to express my needs and my emotions had found the volume button and cranked it up. The beauty of finding that all of you is welcome, of receiving an invitation into a house where you don't have to carve bits off or silence certain voices to be accepted was breathtakingly powerful and heart-achingly difficult. It was like I was having to learn the colours all over again; that maybe green was not green after all - maybe it was red, or blue, or pink.

The rules didn't work, and the space was sacred... but the home with the sign reading 'NO NEEDY PEOPLE ALLOWED' was one I had lived in for many years and in many relationships - and one I knew I was going back to.

Disagreeing with an agreement you have lived with for a long time takes more than wisdom, it takes courage too. Experiencing a home that feels like freedom is one thing, but going back to the home that you live in day to day that still has all these written and unwritten rules in now feels smaller, like it shrank whilst you were gone.

The pioneer at this point has to figure out whether the house with the labels and the rules is the place they want to live in, or whether they are brave enough to carve a new path. The pioneer now has to decide whether they shrink into the small house or whether the uncharted ground is calling louder. The pioneer knows that there are good things in this house, they don't want to leave altogether but somewhere a desire for more spaciousness calls them to take hold of the door handle and gaze for a moment at the wide open space outside. It causes them to wonder if something else is possible; if there is new ground that the earth is crying out for them to explore.

My first pioneer step was to recognise the rules of the house. The second step was to claim that this house and all it's do's and don'ts was stifling me. The sad reality is that too many marriages, friendships and connections are abandoned at this point. It can be hard to see a new path when we see how we are being stifled and so we jump ship and call it a day instead of stepping out onto new ground to create something else.

As I look back at the path I have walked over the last six months I see that it has taken me somewhere beautiful. I see the small house back in the distance and I reflect on the years I lived there, shrunken but secure. It was there I learned many things. I learned the rules, but it was also there that I learned which rules to break in order to thrive. I allow the memory of this home to pause in my mind for a moment, and I don't resent it anymore because now I stand in a wide spacious place. And I maybe smile a little when I see how far I have come.

In this place I get to have needs, and I get to express them to those I love. In this place I feel deeply and widely, in this place there are tears very often and those tears are welcomed and celebrated. On this path 'needy' is a indication that I long to connect, to have those I can be dependent on and those who can depend on me. Somehow, here I am not weaker by expressing my needs but stronger. I can now ask for things from my husband when I need them without feeling like a burden or a child. When he chooses to meet a need it builds the bond between us - being needed is now a strength we offer each, other not a weakness Looking back I realise we have pioneered new ground.

I now get to offer this new ground to those in my world - some love it and celebrate it, others are some what puzzled by the whole sloppy mess, others sneer and turn away and all of that is okay because here I have found a space I can thrive in, a space I can breathe in. Here there are no labels or signs over the door that cause me to shrink down or carve pieces off. Here I get to be me with all my needs and here 'ALL OF ME IS WELCOME!'

The journey to new ground has several steps to take:

- Recognise the rules of the house you're in - have you seen those 'In this house...' signs that you can buy to put on your wall? They say things like 'in this house we love well, have fun, etc'. They often say more about what we hope for than about the reality. If you were to make a real one with all the weird wonky rules you abide by - I suspect it would look quite different!
- Recognise whether these rules honour your values and cause you to thrive, or dishonour them causing you to shrink and disconnect.
- See if you have made any agreements that you realise you don't actually agree with or want to agree with. This could be an agreement like 'needy is bad' or 'you should always toe the line' or around a relationship stance like 'men should be providers' or 'I should be married by now' or one of a million more.
- If you're shrinking you have to decide whether you want to live in a house with all these unwritten rules or whether you want something new.
- If you want something new you need to lean into your pioneer DNA in order to claim a new path, to find new ground.
- Then it is one foot after the other, step by faltering step until you find yourself in a new space which you can name and claim.

Rarely are the rules you have agreed with common to only one space, although they can be. I realised I could express my needs and emotions in very few spaces, and walking out this new pioneer path is easier in some relationships than in others, but I have a deep seated determination that I have named and claimed and will keep on walking out for the purpose of freedom, thriving and deep connection.

The following exercise is one that will help you to recognise the rules of the houses you're in: in your relationships, organisations and within yourself. Start with one place you feel a sense of discontentment in, but you can use this process over and over. You, my Beautiful Pioneer, can carve out as many untrodden pathways in as many relationships as you can; there is so much ground to uncover, so much to explore. So use this tool, then use it again and again for the purpose of freedom and deep connection.

So choose one of of the 'homes' from your relational wheel…

You are going to go through some questions in order to explore the house you are in, and maybe discover places which don't match up to your values. I have very quickly mapped out my experience below as an example, and an empty set of questions can be found on the next page for you to journal through. I encourage you to use as much detail as you can… this is my brief summary of a much longer set of answers!

JOURNAL TIME

Which 'home' from your relational wheel are you starting with?
My marriage

What is the sign over the door that sums up
the unwritten rules you are struggling with?
NO NEEDY PEOPLE ALLOWED

What are some of these unwritten rules?
Be self-sufficient, don't show weakness or needs.

What causes you to feel stuck or stifled here?
I can't fully be myself, I have to pretend.

What new ground would you love to pioneer and explore?
A place where all of me in welcome.

What agreements do you need to disagree with in order
to pioneer something new in this relationship?
Being needy causes disconnection not connection.

JOURNAL TIME

Which 'home' from your relational wheel are you starting with?

What is the sign over the door that sums up the unwritten rules you are struggling with?

What are some of these unwritten rules?

What causes you to feel stuck or stifled here?

JOURNAL TIME

*What new ground would you love to pioneer
and explore?*

*What agreements do you need to disagree with in
order to pioneer something new in this relationship?*

CHAPTER 8:
THE GREEN BLOB
OF CONNECTION...
choosing to pay the price

A while ago I realised I was having constant issues with the calendar on my phone. I have a calendar that syncs from my laptop to my phone because no two days look the same in my world and if I didn't have a calendar that pinged at me 30 minutes before an appointment I would be a scheduling disaster! Because I know this about myself, I am hot at putting everything into my phone, whether it's a client, a coffee with a friend or date night with my husband. For some reason I found myself in the strange position where I kept missing appointments or looking at my calendar, knowing I had put an appointment in, but finding it empty.

A week or so earlier I'd had a message come in from my mobile phone provider telling me that I had used up my quota of monthly data. In order to not to be charged for Facebook status updates flying in every two seconds, I had swiped the little green blob on my phone that disconnected the apps from the internet because in all honesty I was not willing to pay any money to know that someone's cat had vomited on their rug.

Without realising it I had disconnected my calendar from its ability to sync with my laptop so I was glibly adding appointments onto one device which were not appearing when they needed to on another. Apparently clever apps, which make my day-to-day life happen, don't work if they are not connected properly! I realised there was a price I needed to pay in order to reconnect in a way that made my life work.

Our relationships are not so different. We have to be willing to pay a price in order to restore connection if we want our relationships to work well, if we want to be in sync. Too often we have unwittingly swiped the little green blob of disconnection because we are not willing to step up to the cost associated with keeping the 'app' working well. Where do you have a connection that needs to be invested in? Where are you facing a disconnection issue because you have swiped the green blob and are refusing to pay the price?

Eden was the place where true connection was modelled - where relationship with each other and relationship with the Divine were uninterrupted. No green blobs swiped there thank you! That place of connection was affected when humans decided to ignore the advice of the Manufacturer and to make up their own way as they went along - they thought they knew best. If you don't know the rest of the bible, it is basically the story of God reconnecting with his beloved. Sadly many people don't know that this is the major plot line, but the long and short of it is that the Creator loved his greatest creation so very deeply that he would rather die than be disconnected. Bold stuff. And his method of payment?

Love.

Let me explain a little. Later on in the story, God hands out commandments to his people. The word 'commandment' conjures up thoughts of an authority figure handing out an edict, but the word used *entole* comes from two old Hebrew words *en* and *telos*: *en* meaning in and *telos* which means to focus and work towards the end result. A commandment is basically a way of placing purposeful focus on an intended outcome; it's not about being told what to do. We are told that the greatest commandment is simple - to love God, others and ourselves. It tells us at we were built with love in mind. It tells us that every aspect of our inner selves - our heart (inner life, intention, character, centre), our soul (seat of affections, will, distinct identity) and mind (intellect, understanding, insight) were placed within us in order for us to love and thus fulfil our purpose in the world. It tells us that in order to be focusing on and working towards the end result, we must love well. The greatest commandment is love and this was the green blob of connection used in Eden and after.

The bible is the account of the way we have been loved as humans - we are not loved simply in words, but in thought and action. There are certain things we can glean from this intricate several-thousand year old storyline. Now, I recognise that some of you may be unfamiliar with the God of the bible so I will use the metaphor he uses a lot to describe the way he thinks of himself in relationship with us. He uses the analogy of being a Father. The example he sets is the one of being an epic dad who deeply wants his kids to know they are loved in order for them to grow up healthy and well connected. How does he do this?

1. It says that our Divine Dad loved us before we learnt to behave well, whether we love him back, whether we change or not. He seems to love us good and bad; his love is unconditional.
2. He envisions who we could be - past the broken grotty bits to a place where we are our true self. He sees our lost glory.
3. He approaches us with tenderness and kindness.
4. He delights in us - not only in who we can become but he seems to delight in us whilst we are still in process.
5. He gently disrupts the grotty in us in order to create more space for life.
6. His love is always laced with forgiveness.

The One who dreamed up Eden chose to be known by an intimate relational term - Father - and the way he connects with us and asks us to connect with others and ourselves well is through the example above.

These six things are game changers. If we held even one or two well in our relationships with each other we would start to find heaven on earth. The truth is that there is a price to pay for this type of relationship; there is a cost to the green blob of connection.

There is a cost to loving unconditionally, there is a cost to seeing past people's grotty to their glory, there is a cost to choosing tenderness and kindness, to delighting in people especially when they are in process, there is a cost to lovingly disrupting people for the purpose of bringing more life. There is a cost associated with building deep connection.

I love this quote from Mother Teresa:

> "The greatest disease in the West today is not TB or leprosy; it is being unwanted, unloved, and uncared for. We can cure physical diseases with medicine, but the only cure for loneliness, despair, and hopelessness is love. There are many in the world who are dying for a piece of bread but there are many more dying for a little love. The poverty in the West is a different kind of poverty -- it is not only a poverty of loneliness but also of spirituality. There's a hunger for love, as there is a hunger for God."

> *'A Simple Path'* Ballantine Books, 1995.

So many relationships, particularly in Western culture, are poverty stricken because we are not willing to invest in other people in a way that costs us: we simply don't make the hard decision to pay the cost associated with loving well. How can we expect relationships to be right if we assign them little or no value? Love has several attributes: it is patient, kind, void of envy, does not insist on its own way, is not irritable or resentful, it pursues and rejoices in truth, it bears with, believes in, hopes for and endures. The cost to swipe the green blob of connection is the cost of offering these things - it is the choice to be selfless and love deeply.

If you look back at the list of six things offered as an example above, the thread is the removal of self; if you are a parent yourself you will know this journey. It starts the first moment your baby screams and you sacrifice your sleep for its full belly. Parents choose to pay the price because they are being screamed at until 3am, well, that and this peculiar parental bond of course! But each of our relationships need the same level of sacrifice of self on behalf of another if they are going to be relationships that stay connected and thrive.

In Western culture we are told to focus on me first; the culture of Eden is *other* focused. In Eden we love without placing conditions on that love, we love by looking under the grotty to the glory of another, we offer tenderness, kindness and delight whilst someone is changing growing and becoming. Mother Teresa modelled this kind of love to the underclass of India, a group of people who were deemed to be unlovable.

She modelled the patient, kind, self-less, hopeful love that manifests itself in more than word but in thought and action also.

Mother Teresa offered Eden to those who others offered nothing to. Of course there was a cost; you cannot offer this type of love and not pay a price. The same is true of the love offered from the God of Eden - it was a love that cost a great deal - and the cost was personal.

If you and I want to build relationships that are truly loving and life giving, there will be a green blob of connection to swipe - and there will be a price associated with this. The price of connection is usually self; it is a choice to be other focused, the love like a Mother or a Father who chooses another's belly over their sleep. This type of love is countercultural and it is a game changer. This type of love is one that casts out relational poverty, loneliness, despair and hopelessness at great personal cost; knowing that the other is worth it. The amazing truth is that when we offer this type of love, it starts to come back our way bit by bit - we start to be loved as we love others.

The choice we each have is to take a long hard look at our 'credit' and see where it is going. Who gets your heart, your time, your forgiveness, your patience? Who gets your kindness and your choice to see the best in them? Who gets the best you? Sadly, the truth for many of us is that strangers get a better deal than those closest to us; colleagues at work are offered more relational credit than spouses; parents and siblings get the pence left at the bottom of your purse - those who should receive the best of us often get the dregs after we have spent our credit elsewhere.

They say affairs don't begin in the bedroom. They begin with that extra bit of kindness that you don't offer at home, that little bit more patience or hopefulness or conversation. Affairs begin when more credit is offered to another, than to the one you previously pledged to.

Our loved ones deserve more than the dregs; they deserve the best and the most we have to offer. The choice we have is whether to place credit where it's due. So go back to the settings, swipe the green blob and pay the price that is needed to change the game.

Don't ignore that insistent nudge pointing to a relationship that is becoming poverty-stricken. It's not too late to choose to invest, to love in thought, word and deed, to be the game changer in a relationship that is offline and not functioning.

Which relationship is feeling a little poverty stricken? Come up with ideas below of how you could invest in real practical ways in order to turn the tide and build a deeper connection.

JOURNAL TIME

1. Love unconditionally – go first!

2. See past their grotty to their glory.

3. Offer tenderness and kindness.

JOURNAL TIME

4. Delight in - even when in process.

5. Only disrupt the grotty to give more space for life.

6. Offer love that is always laced with forgiveness.

CHAPTER 9:

COME OUT
OF HIDING...

unravel the shroud of shame

Several years ago I was invited to speak at a women's conference. I have done a fair amount of public speaking and other than the standard nerves I am not easily phased or daunted by the prospect but for this event, I was in pieces. The title of the talk they ask me to give was 'You are Beautiful'. And therein lay the problem. Give me a talk about life change, moving forwards well, being the best version of you - I can do all of that; but speaking on beauty was unnerving me because I realised how uncomfortable I was with the topic.

Now, years later, I recognise that the word beauty triggered something buried deep within me concerning my imperfections and my own shame with regards to my physical self and the construct of beauty which pervades our western culture. I didn't feel beautiful and so talking to others around the topic of beauty unearthed deep feelings of inadequacy.

When I think about beauty, I land with the conclusion of being not good enough. Beautiful people should speak about beauty, and I don't hold enough beauty to measure up. I did the math - and something wasn't right.

The more I tried to prepare this talk the more I realised that there was a wound I was carrying that went deeper than I had known. I realised this wound affected the way I saw myself, but it also affected the way I showed up with other people, how I behaved in my marriage, how I chose to perceive others. I realised I was ashamed of this wound, of being not enough and my strategy was to cover and hide. I realised that I had become a master at hiding.

The narrative I told myself over and over was that I needed to hide the parts of myself that weren't all that pretty. It was the good and right thing to do. My body post-pregnancy was not what it used to be, I was tipping the scales at 'overweight' and had a weird post c-section middle that I had no idea how to cover over well - unless I had layers of cardigans and scarves. I had pinned all my shame on my post-baby body for several years but writing this talk made me realise that nothing much had changed with the c-section. I realised that hiding parts of myself was actually not new ground for me; I had been hiding the 'uglies' as long as I could remember. I'd not had it brought to my attention in such a physical way before, but at some point between childhood and adulthood I had learnt a lesson from somewhere that uglies should be hidden.

This talk was a turning point for me in beginning to realise that shame was a real and present issue in my life and that covering and hiding was not actually helping. I saw clearly that staying hidden was only multiplying my shame and that covering over was causing the wounds to fester underneath.

I remembered what was written about humans in Eden - they were naked, and they felt no shame. In Eden, man and woman were naked. They were fully on show, fully seen, uncovered. Being naked was a gift Adam and Eve offered to each other in order to have a thriving relationship. And they felt no shame about it.

Being naked is vulnerable - choosing to unclothe yourself so that you can be seen is a brave and tender stance. The word 'vulnerable' comes from the Latin word *vulnus* meaning 'wound', which later became the Old English word meaning 'able to be wounded'. When you are naked you are vulnerable because you are laying yourself open to another and placing the risk of being wounded into their hands; of course you are also placing the risk of being loved, accepted and seen in their hands too. In fact, full unclothed vulnerability is what we are craving from our loved ones, and what we wish we could offer them. As humans, we yearn to be seen for who we truly are; it is how we were designed to love and be loved.

Intimacy is what happens when two people choose to be vulnerable; it is a mutual choice to be fully seen - we are told that 'they' were naked, not just one of them. Until we choose to become uncovered we cannot find true deep connection and intimacy.

In our culture we have simmered intimacy down to sex and we are missing out on a whole world of intimacy that humans were created to experience. Sharing your naked body through sex is widely acceptable in the West, and yet it seems that sharing your naked soul with another person is more of an issue. We know how to be naked, but we don't know how to be truly intimate and authentically vulnerable; instead we learn to offer covered or cloaked intimacy at risk of being wounded.

My tendency to hide my body was covering a fear of being wounded. I desired intimacy and vulnerability but I didn't need a dictionary definition or Latin root word for me to know that this was a risky business that meant I could get hurt. This went way deeper than a c-section scar.

We cannot thrive unless we feel deep connection with others, and the key to that connection is the willingness to be seen. You cannot be seen if you are always self-protecting and covering. It just cannot happen. 'Naked' is the key to connection.

We get a glimpse of the moment that coverings became the norm for mana and woman in the story of Eden. They chose disconnection and they felt shame; once they felt shame the first thing they did was hide themselves.

At this point it's worth stopping and looking at shame. Shame is rife in our culture partly because we do not understand it properly and partly because we live in a world whose weapon of choice is the ability to shrink someone down when we feel that we don't measure up. 'Shame on you' is our culture's mantra.

Now, we all have uglies. You may be the most beautiful creature on the planet - you still have blemishes somewhere. We all have imperfections in our physical bodies, in our temperament, in our personalities and with our inter-personal skills and ability to connect. We all say things about others behind their backs that are ugly, or think thoughts that are blemished, and we feel guilty about those things that we have done wrong. That is normal and healthy.

Shame is a level deeper and simmers under the waters of 'guilty'.

Shame sees the uglies and translates them from imperfections to deep core flaws and results in the messages 'I am bad', 'I am flawed', 'I am not enough'. It is the difference between 'I feel guilty for what I *do*' and 'I feel shame for who I *am*.' It is not guilt that causes us to hide, it is shame. The sad reality of life is that we claim shame much more readily than we claim responsibility.

The example set for us in Eden is to come out of hiding.

This has so much less to do with physical unveiling than internal unveiling, but for you, as with me, there may be a connection. We are self-sabotaging our relationships because of a narrative that tells us that if we fully show up we will get wounded.

Now, please hear me. There are situations you absolutely should not put yourself in. If you are being bullied or abused by another, you need to ask for help by a professional as to how to walk out of any space where power is being held over you in an unhealthy or damaging way.

For many, old wounds are keeping us hidden in good, healthy relational places. If you desire deep connection, you have to come out of hiding and be seen. It's time to peel off a layer of protection, lose a cardigan or a scarf. If you feel guilty, there may be apologies to make or conversations to have - this is a great way of stepping out into the open. If you know you have a blemish, sharing this with a trusted friend and asking for help is an unveiling of your true self. Don't let unspoken guilt keep you hiding in unwarranted shame. Asking for what you need is vulnerable - it's a layer off.

We need to change the messages we have received and accepted that holding shame is a better option than admitting guilt. We choose to wallow in the murky underbelly of shame when we could simply admit where we have been at fault, apologise and find freedom. It takes a willingness to come out of hiding.

We all have those friends who are so guarded and covered that we just cannot get past a superficial level of friendship because we just cannot see the 'real' them. We all want to be fully seen and fully known, and loved when our true self is seen; yet more often than not we are the ones choosing not to be seen by letting the voice of shame speak so loudly in our life.

So - where are you hiding? What are you covering?

I invite you to picture an Egyptian mummy. I am placing in your hand the edge of a bandage which is the shrouding which keeps us bound and dead. Somewhere inside of you there is someone who wants to thrive and you cannot thrive if you are shrouded. These bandages are the shrouding of shame and it is time to start to unravel them.

This talk I was asked to give was the first step in my unravelling. As I stood before a room of women speaking about beauty I was choosing to loosen my shrouds. When the voice of life becomes louder than the voice of shame we start to breathe again. Little by little the bandages unravel and something new begins. Life can start again.

Your soul will come to life when you let the things you have covered yourself with start to unravel. Coping can seem like a good idea, but it's not a patch on thriving. Come out of hiding and into an open space to find life and freedom from shame. Do the hard work of separating guilt and shame - deal with the right one and the other will quieten down. The first thing to do is to recognise the voice of shame. Where do you see the messages of 'I'm not enough', 'I'm flawed' or 'I'm bad or broken' in your life?

It may help to try to finish off these sentences below and then journal around them in the space underneath for a while and see if you can start to locate the place of shame that is in you. Find the edge of that bandage that is keeping you shrouded and maybe start to tug it a little and see what happens when it begins to loosen its hold on you.

This is a biggie, it really is, but you can do this, I know you can because deep down we know that shame is not allowing us to breathe deeply and live fully. Staying hidden does not help us to build intimacy because we cannot be vulnerable if we are wrapped in layers of shame.

JOURNAL TIME

I wish I could be more...

Sometimes I wonder if I'm too...

JOURNAL TIME

I think my loved ones want me to be...

If I came out of hiding more,
I would be different because...

CHAPTER 10:
FINDING YOUR VOICE...
putting down silent assumption

There was once a little girl who loved words. She loved to sing and talk and discuss things. She loved reading stories and writing words down that came into her heart and head. She was never happier than when she was using her voice – it was her greatest tool to love others and feel loved in return. One day someone told her that she used too many words, that her words were annoying to them. The little girl did not understand; words were so beautiful and such an amazing way to love and be loved. And so she carried on singing and speaking and loving and being loved through words.

Some time later someone else said that they did not like the way she used her words, that they were silly and too much. She sensed that when she used her words in a way that felt natural like breathing to her, other people did not always feel so loved. She started to doubt herself, to question what she had always thought was easy as one, two, three and as natural as breathing. She started to filter herself, to question her words, to stop them bubbling out like a joyful brook just in case what was easy and natural was actually annoying and too much. It became hard to know what was right and wrong, whether up was actually down and left was in fact right – or maybe wrong. The more she filtered and stopped the brook bubbling the less she sang and talked and discussed. And the less she sang and talked and discussed the less she loved and felt love. She had learnt to doubt her greatest tool and so she put it down and slowly her voice became silent. Every now and again the brook would bubble over and her voice would come back to life, but the doubts would creep in once more and she would choose to put her voice away just in case she was annoying with her words.

The little girl became a woman and one day the woman realised she had lost her voice completely. She must have put it down sometime ago but because of the filtering and doubting she had used it less and less and so she hadn't noticed that somewhere along her journey it had gotten lost. The woman could no longer use her voice to give love and receive love so she had to try to find other tools, silent tools. She tried many things and gradually she learnt to live and love without words. Sometime later, the woman discovered a new tool that she could use in place of her words. It was not such a joyful tool, it was not as easy as one, two, three or as natural as the bubbling brook but after a while this tool seemed to fill some of the void she experienced from having lost her voice. This tool was called 'assumption' and she realised she could use it even though she was silent; in fact it seemed to work better that way.

There was once a woman who grew to use the only tool she had left, once she had lost her voice, in order to fill the gap with the people she wanted to love - the tool of silent assumption.

Several years later this woman had become very skilled with her new tool; she used it often and easily and it had become as easy as one, two, three and almost as natural as a bubbling brook. But the woman was not happy. Her life seemed hard and complicated and small, and she tried really hard to make people understand what she felt or hoped for or needed - but often they used the tool of silent assumption as well and one, two, three became other numbers that didn't add up. 'If only I could find my voice' she thought to herself, 'then I could tell them what I really want, who I really am and what I really need - and I could ask them what they really want and who they really are and what they really need.'

As soon as she thought this, she remembered back to the people who had told her that they didn't love her words and that she used them too often. She felt shame that her words had not been seen as the gift she thought they were, she remembered all the times she had sung and spoken and discussed without even thinking about whether they should have been filtered, and her shame grew. 'That must have been for children' she thought, 'no-one would love me if I started to use my words again. I wouldn't even know how and would make a fool of myself for even trying'.

She carried on using the tool of silent assumption as the fear of using her words was too much for her to try. Until the day came when the fear was no longer greater than her sadness at having lost her voice. That day she saw a little girl singing and talking and discussing, using her words so freely and unfiltered; as easy as one, two, three and as joyfully as a bubbling brook. A tear rolled down the cheek of the woman as she remembered how much she had loved her voice before she doubted. Another tear rolled as she realised just how much her voice had meant to her before any other voices silenced her. All of a sudden the woman knew that silent assumption was not good enough any more and that her voice must be found.

She journeyed back to the place she last remembered using the beautiful tool of her words and after much searching she found her voice laying abandoned on the ground. As she held it, she could feel the familiarity of it alongside the fear of wondering if she could remember how it worked and the memory of people who did not love her tool as much as she did. She gingerly tried her words out - quietly, croaking a little, she used her voice. A word, a phrase, a sentence. A thought, an idea, a whisper.

She began to use her voice to say what she felt. She began to ask for what she needed. She invited others to do the same to her - to use their voices back. She realised that many people liked the tool of silent assumption and were curious about the use of her voice, but she knew that staying silent was no longer an option for her. This beautiful gift was back in her hands and heart; her voice had been found.

It took some time for her to fully remember the sound of her voice and how to use it well without it squeaking or croaking. Sometimes she stayed silent a little too long, other times her words burst out a little quickly like the bubbling brook over-running; but over time she learnt to use this amazing tool again and before long she was singing and talking and discussing almost as easy as one, two, three.

Every now and again she would meet someone who offered her silent assumption and she would be tempted to do the same. However, she allowed herself to remember the joy of her words, the freedom they offered her and the way that they were her greatest tool for giving and receiving love. She dared to keep using them even when it scared her or she worried what the other person would think.

This is the story of those who realised that finding your voice can be scary but that silent assumption will never be the best tool for giving or receiving love.

....

On paper, silent assumption is ridiculous! How could we think that making an assumption about someone without checking it out or communicating it to them in any way could be better than actually discussing it? How could we think it is preferable to tell ourselves a narrative about what someone else is thinking, their motives or reasons for doing something, their heart or intentions, than to ask them? Crazy town! But we all do it, right? We make assumptions and we act like they are the gospel truth when they may be far from it. We confuse silent assumption with spoken agreement and our connections are being poisoned because of this misunderstanding.

The problem with silent assumptions in any relationship is that they offer a narrow perspective when it comes to possibility. In the place of silent assumption we often land with a 'truth' that something cannot be changed, will not happen, won't be accepted or welcomed and will probably fail.

It can be hard to learn to voice our needs, desires, dreams and hopes for our future and relationships but it does open up fresh possibility and a wider perspective - it's like turning the telescope around the right way. The view is always wider when you use your words.

We have all had times when our voices were not welcomed. We have all bumbled around tricky conversations where we have said too much or said something silly. We have all felt bruised when we voiced something that wasn't received well or was argued down - but your voice is still a better tool than silent assumption for building relationship well. Even when it's hard or clumsy, it is worth the effort to push through the discomfort to learn to use this your voice more wisely and more eloquently.

Somewhere in you is a bubbling brook of hopes, desires, dreams and needs that are desperate to come out in a place where they will be celebrated as joyful and beautiful, where they don't have to be perfect or make total sense, where they can be real and true and from the heart. You can be the one in a relationship who goes first.

You can start a revolution of choosing to move away from silent assumption and instead to use your voice to verbalise what is present for you in your relationships, at work, with your kids - wherever you are. It may take a while for this to catch on, but you will be able to inspire others to try it out as well - when you do it, you will inspire others.

Let's try it out here as a first step to unleashing the beautiful bubbling brook.

Choose four people or places where you feel 'silenced' in someway - where fear or shame or something else means you have lost your voice and you are not saying what you need, want, dream of, or hope for. As always, the relationship wheel is there to help you. For each relationship I invite you to finish the three prompts without the fear of how they will be received, or overthinking how to say them. In this space you don't need to filter or manage what you say - you get to practice the 'bubbling over' of not needing to get it right. In each of the boxes, identify who or where you want to focus on at the top and then the three things you want to use your voice to say underneath.

The next step of course would be to go on the journey of finding and using your voice with these actual real life people in actual real life... but I'll leave that with you! I trust that one day the fear will no longer be greater than the sadness at having lost your voice and that the bubbling brook will invite and inspire beautiful, honest and life giving conversations.

JOURNAL TIME

Which pie piece? ....

1. What I really need from you is:

2. I really want you to know that:

3. In our relationship I have made the assumption that:

Which pie piece? ....

1. What I really need from you is:

2. I really want you to know that:

3. In our relationship I have made the assumption that:

JOURNAL TIME

Which pie piece? ....

1. *What I really need from you is:*

2. *I really want you to know that:*

3. *In our relationship I have made the assumption that:*

Which pie piece? ....

1. *What I really need from you is:*

2. *I really want you to know that:*

3. *In our relationship I have made the assumption that:*

CHAPTER 11:

YOUR SKIRT IS IN YOUR KNICKERS...

knowing your blindspots

One thing you should know about me is that I am the girl that awkward things tend to happen to. I am the girl who trips walking on a stage or has food dripped down their top. I am the girl who fell down a man-hole (actually true) and who sang loudly at the quiet bit in my son's school carol concert and got sniggered at by eight year old boys. I'm just that girl.

My all-time embarrassing moment was when I was on holiday one year. We were going out for the evening so I'd done my hair and make up (which is not all that common - usually I just roll straight from bed to the school run) and I put on a sweet skirt I had bought with a cute strappy top. I had a bit of a tan going on and felt pretty dang good. We went to the bar for a drink as the sun set across the ocean, it was a beautiful evening and as I got up to take a photograph a woman scurried pretty quickly behind me and whispered in my ear 'Your skirt is in your knickers…' AWKWARD MOMENT. I thanked her profusely as I frantically batted at the back of my skirt in order to untuck and recover an ounce of dignity. Thank the Lord I had good knickers on and a bit of a tan!

It's a memory I laugh at but it also became a picture of a greater issue in my life. Too often I walk around with a blindspot about myself relationally; I have a flaw that I can't see as I merrily wander through life, unaware that my skirt is tucked into my knickers.

One of the first things I thought after that woman came and saved me from my own ridiculous self was 'How long have I been walking round like that?!' Just how many men, women and children got to see my underwear before someone had the courage to come over and tell me I was making a bit of a fool of myself? I was pretty mortified but I could have kissed that woman who saved me from wandering around with an embarrassing blindspot all evening!

A few years ago I was working for a church and my line manager called me into his office one day. We chatted about how things were then we had a 'do you know your skirt is in your knickers?' conversation (not literally this time, I'm pleased to report). With real tenderness and love he told me how sometimes I showed up with real passive-aggressive energy. There were times I was 'Happy Helen' - I was helpful, kind, patient, encouraging and then 'Grumpy Helen' would take over and I would become sour, silently aggressive, difficult and moody. He just called it out and showed me a blindspot.

As he said it, I knew he was absolutely right - I knew I could be that person, I just hadn't realised everyone else saw her as well. I was pretty embarrassed and I noticed in that moment I had a desire to explain myself, to give excuses why I had been 'Grumpy Helen' that day or to that person. I wanted to find mitigating circumstances - I was the Queen of 'Yeah, but…'.

But I knew he was right and because I knew he was putting himself on the line to say this (the wrath of 'Grumpy Helen' was not something you wished upon yourself, believe me), I could take that he was only saying this for my good.

My choice in that moment was to either protect my pride, refuse to take responsibility and fight back because I was embarrassed that he had called out my blindspot, or to swallow my pride, untuck my skirt and thank him for his courage at telling me the hard truth about me and the way I showed up.

I can guarantee you that there are areas in your life where you have been walking round with your skirt tucked in your knickers (or whatever the boy equivalent is) for years or maybe even decades. I can also guarantee you that countless people have seen your blindspot - your underwear has been on show. It's kind of mortifying to think of but we often fear people's perceptions of us enough that we hold back on saying the hard truth in love.

It might be someone told you the hard truth but because you didn't have enough relational credit with them, or they said it badly, you threw out the truth about your underwear too quickly. Feedback can be your friend - whether it is given well or not. Having the wisdom to know if it is true or someone else's nonsense being thrown at you is a gift. So how do we do that?

Well, the easiest way is to practice. If you can practice in a carved-out safe environment then you are more likely to filter and sieve the truth in a real life conversation.

The way to practice it, is to invite it. Gulp.

I know, I know… it's crazy hard and makes you sweat and get uncomfortable but believe me - knowing your skirt is in your knickers is a gift in the long run; knowing the truth about your blindspots will set you free.

The best way you can discover your blindspots is to invite someone you trust to sit with you to help you to 'see' things you haven't been able to before. For this one you are going to have to be crazy-brave and invite someone else into the process if you haven't done so already. Gulp again.

Asking questions such as…

Where do you see I am not growing or progressing in a certain relationship?

Where do you think I am stuck?

What could I change?

Or simply...

Where do I have a blindspot? or

What is it like to live on the other side of me? - asking your kids or spouse that one is a fun Sunday afternoon hobby!

If you trust the heart of the person you are conversing with, their honesty will be a blessing to you. I promise.

And you will need to self-manage your reaction a whole lot. I promise that too.

The truth is that when we are caught with our skirt in our knickers we want to deflect, blame or shame our way out of the embarrassment we feel. It's why so few people take responsibility for their actions - it's easier to blame someone else. When we don't deflect, blame or shame - we have the opportunity to really honestly look at ourselves and our blindspots and integrate them so that we can grow and develop. We expect our kids to learn this lesson - we teach them what it looks like to take responsibility for their actions without blaming someone else - but they have learnt from the masters. As adults we are usually pretty adept at blaming someone else when we could take responsibility without the deflection, blame or shame.

It's a lie that you are perfect, and it's a lie that you are supposed to be, but those lies underpin the desire to deflect, blame or shame our way out of the blindspots we have.

So self-awareness and self-management are key. How do you usually react to feedback? What are the internal scripts you have for when someone criticises you? How do you deflect, blame or shame your way out of an uncomfortable conversation or situation? For me, I like to offer a list of justifications as to why my actions were valid, and in doing so attached some of the blame to another person. What are your 'go to's'? Maybe jot a few down here...

Once you know how you deflect, you will be able to manage the 'Yeah, but...' which will probably creep up (or maybe fly out at speed and with life-destroying vengeance rather than creep...just me?!) The truth is we have all had 'feedback' given well or badly and it makes a difference to how it is received. But even badly given feedback can be a gift to you if there is some truth in it.

We cannot change the way feedback is given, we can only change the heart we receive it with. That is our responsibility.

So set yourself up to succeed. Assess how you take feedback now, invite someone in who loves you and will offer it well - and if in doubt have chocolate nearby to shovel into your mouth to stop you deflecting when you're tempted to 'Yeah, but...' instead of receiving the truth. You're welcome for that little tip.

The more you can invite people in to untuck your skirt with you, the better you will handle feedback when it is thrown at you laced with anger or fear or unfairness. It will give you tools to deal with your emotionally unhealthy boss or friend or parent whose 'feedback' has ended up causing you deep wounds because of how it was said. You are setting yourself up for a win.

It may also help you to have a handy little phrases like 'Thank you for your feedback. I will go and think about it'. These give you the space to assess the feedback more objectively in a way where you get to sift for gold without throwing back a 'Yeah, but...'. It will give you a pause for your hackles to go down a little so you are not triggered in the moment.

So be brave, send a text to your buddy, buy some chocolate and ask the bold question 'where can't I see that my skirt is tucked in my knickers?' I've left space for you to write down whatever is helpful out of this conversation (or more than one conversation if you're super brave!). You may find that you want to think about a next step to help you grow or things you want to clarify or practice. Note where you wanted to deflect, blame or shame and how you best dealt with this (or not!) and what you would want to do differently moving forwards.

JOURNAL TIME

Where can't I see that my skirt is tucked in my knickers?

JOURNAL TIME

*Now I know some of my blindspots,
what else could I do differently?
What new things could I try?*

CHAPTER 12:

STUCK IN THE MIDDLE WITH YOU...

the messy middle place

Being in the middle is the strangest, weirdest, hardest place. Being in the middle is knowing you are no longer in the 'what has been' but that you are not yet in the 'what is to come'. When you are stuck in the middle you cannot go back and yet you cannot move forward. The middle is not an easy place because it can often feel like it is filled with frustration, confinement and confusion. In the middle is where we get tired and demotivated.

I remember being newly married, figuring out what it looked and felt like to be a wife. We started to build a home and a marriage, took trips and explored together, fought over where pans would go in the kitchen and how to be two different people in one. We spent several years just the two of us working on becoming a married couple... this was the 'what has been'. I remember the high of getting pregnant. We had been planning a family for a while so when it finally happened we were over the moon. I remember ringing my parents and telling my in laws in their sitting room, seeing Dave's dad tear up over the prospect of his little boy having a little one of his own... being pregnant was the 'what is to come'.

Between those two places was the middle, the long hard gestation period of waiting. In the middle was the leaving behind of the old with no guarantee of what the new would hold. The middle was littered with hopes and dreams and visions of the future, and the frustration of not being able to make it happen, to speed up the process, to get to the outcome we desired. In the middle is when you can easily lose hope, become bitter and angry and resentful. In the middle is where we compare and seek out what is right, declaring 'not fair' based on what others get or we seem not to. When you're in the wait, your heart is too soft and too hard and too open and too closed. The middle is a hard place.

It wasn't long before getting pregnant changed from being the 'what is to come'. I remember walking down the hospital corridor holding my gown, conscious of the open gaping back, bare feet on cold floor. I remember bright overhead lights and spinal injections, too many doctors and 'the feeling like someone washing up in your tummy' as my son was pulled from my sectioned belly...becoming a mummy was the 'what is to come'. Between the two was waiting and hoping and soft-hard-open-closed hearts and comparing and wishing. Between the two was the wait in the middle.

I remember becoming a mummy to a baby... the what has been.
I remember the sleepless nights... the what has been.
I remember wishing I could get off this crazy merry go round of never-ending hard work.. the what has been.
I remember getting pregnant again. A little too quickly... the what has been.
I remember thinking how easy one child had been... the what has been.

I see now that the 'what is to come' turns into 'what has been' so very, very quickly; but I remember that when you're in the middle the brakes screech on and the world starts spinning slower, the days seem to go on forever, and you wonder if this season will ever end. The gift of hindsight is not offered in the middle place. I remember the thing I hoped for being disappointing and being the best thing ever. I remember the 'what has been' taking up all the space I had and not being the biggest thing in my world. I remember 'between the two' being the hardest thing of all because I knew the only thing I could do was be in the moment.

The truth about the middle ground is that there are things we can only learn here if we are willing to move past the feelings of frustration and simply stop to notice. The strange thing with humans is that we are very good at looking back, very good at looking forward and very under-rehearsed at being here in the now. It's why we are not good at being stuck in the middle; the middle requires you to be present to what is here in this moment without rushing forwards or reminiscing backwards.

The earth will keep on turning, your life will constantly change. What you wished for will quickly become the thing that you have already finished and between every shift is the middle ground where one thing has been and the other has not yet come. Sometimes the threshold of the middle place is short, so short we hardly notice it or give credit to it. Sometimes we are left in the middle for huge painful lengths of time when it feels like the threshold becomes the final destination and it is the only thing we can see.

The truth is that we are never in just one stage at any given time, we can experience all three simultaneously in different areas of our life:

the what has been: the comfortable known
the middle: the threshold between two places
the what is to come: the new unknown.

It is the way of the earth, the way of the Divine, the way of all we see around us and the way of us as well. Unless a seed falls to the ground, something new cannot be born. The harder truth is that after a seed falls to the ground it has to go underground into a season of waiting - not still a seed, not yet a shoot. The strange and wonderful middle. You may well find yourself in a middle place right now. I suspect we all are. You'll know it because you can name what was and what you hope will be but neither are your current reality. You may have just moved out from home but don't yet feel independent.

You may be engaged, not not married. You may be pregnant with what will be, but are not there yet - literally or metaphorically! You may be separated but not divorced, dating but not exclusive, retired but not finished yet, in the change between careers, or churches, or friendships. You may be in a shift in a relationship - it isn't what it was but you're not sure what it will be yet, facing an empty nest or a space where a loved one is no longer. Maybe the shift is an internal one. There are many, many middles.

The hardest middle I have had to negotiate in recent years was during the toddler years of being a parent. I had two babies 18 months apart and we decided that I would step back from my career to be a full-time mum. In all honesty this was the hardest thing I have ever done. I felt like I had left 'me' behind somewhere, and I was holding on until my life could start again. I know many people thrive on having babies and, being a teacher before this, I thought I would be one, but I STRUGGLED. In all honesty, that three year period is a bit of a blur now, but I remember that I was barely hanging on at the time. Had it not been for some good friends and a very attentive mother-in-law I would have sunk under the waves. I remember everyone around me looking like they were loving playing play-doh and singing nursery rhymes with their little treasures; I wanted to climb into a cupboard and not come out. I would hold on until 6pm when my husband came home from work and took over, and if he was even five minutes late I'd be on the phone hunting him down. This three year transition was a tough one. What's funny is that many people looked from the outside and wished they could transition *to* the place where I was, not *from* it as I did! That is why we should be very careful with our assumptions concerning someone else's journey unless we have been invited to walk that road with them. You never know what path someone is walking unless you're on it; the grass may not be greener on their side. I'm pleased to report that we came out of the toddler years fairly unscathed, my kids seem reasonably well-rounded and I never actually had to climb in a cupboard...

Middle places are tough, but for a moment I would like you to consider where you are in a 'middle'. Notice where you feel like the seed, under the earth, not sure of day or night, up or down.

Once you have identified your middle, stay here a moment longer than you usually would See what is here. Look around your heart and notice the climate here.

Stay here on this threshold, stay on this edge, stay in the middle place. As you stay here notice the gift that the middle offers - hands off what has been but not yet on what is to come; open, empty hands.

Look around you in this place and see what is here.

You may see longing or pain.

Release or resentment.

Hope or hopelessness.

You may notice freedom or chains.

Sadness or joy.

A longing to look back or to look forwards.

Stay here a moment longer, whether you chose this path or it was thrust upon you by chance or fate or the Divine or another. Stay here in the intriguing middle on the threshold edge beyond the territory you know and are familiar with; where you have explored the ground and know the contours of the land. Stay here as you see or sense the new land... maybe you can practically touch it, ready for the taking or maybe it is a mirage that you cannot lay your hand to. Stay in the middle between the known and the unknown. Stay in the tension between the two.

Our temptation is to think ahead about the 'what is to come' in order to find a sense of hope and movement but if we move on too quickly we will miss out on what the middle place has to offer. The middle place is a transition place, it is where we let go of what has been in order to pick up what will be. If you don't recognise you are in transition your hands will be so full of what was that you have no room for what will be.

In the middle is where you have empty, hopeful hands. The middle place is an edge between this and that, it marks a place of new territory. The middle place is a threshold, not in and yet not out. And it tends to happen in the dark underground where the seed breaks open in order to become something more.

This process of stopping and letting go whilst feeling like a buried seed has a name. It's called grief. Grief is the beautiful tender threshold of change that moves us from what has been, opening up the space for the new thing to shoot through the peaty soil and reach towards the light. Grief does not have to be a negative thing. This is the lie of our Western culture that keeps us stuck and causes us to hold on to the old dead thing, stopping us from moving forwards. Grief is a gift offered to us in transition. Grief is the permission to stop and notice whilst letting our heart feel all it needs to. Grief is hard and painful and complicated, but a gift nonetheless. In our culture we have no category for gifts which are anything other than comfortable, easy and nice. Grief breaks down the walls of these boxes to teach us something new.

I wish I'd had the permission to grieve my old life before I had kids but the shame I felt that I needed to grieve stopped me. I mean what sort of mother needs to grieve the time she had before her children?! In the absence of healthy grief I felt buried, not planted. I could not appreciate what was here because I was gripping on to what had gone. I couldn't enjoy the now because I was lost in the past. Had I grieved the freedom I had felt before becoming a mum, the sense of identity which I had lost and my space, sleep and rest, who knows what new thing could have grown?

Instead I hunkered down and coped until the season shifted and I could plant something new. I don't have many regrets but I do regret how little I thrived during those three years.

I choose to take that sadness and sow it into the middles I am now in. I refuse to let shame stop me from grieving when I need to, even if other people don't understand why I need to. I take that season and let it teach me that open-handedness and a soft-hard-closed-open heart may be tricky but it is a gift to the thing that is waiting to grow just a season away.

Open your hands and be in the place of grieving. We are going to slow the pace right down now... take the gift of the world spinning slower to see what is here in an area of your life which is a middle. As we slow down, ponder and meditate on each question and let your heart guide you as you start to see what is here for you in your middle.

JOURNAL TIME

Where are you in a middle?
Name 'what has been' and 'what is to come' so that you
can identify the place between the two.
Does the middle have a name?

What are you struggling to let go of from the 'what has been'
in order to be open-handed?

What needs to be said or felt
in order to grieve the last place well?

JOURNAL TIME

What do you appreciate about the middle?

What do you NOT appreciate about the middle?

What do you need here?

Let's stay with the image of the seed waiting in the soil. The best soil that causes the seed to grow well is fertile, weed-free and well-watered.

Fertiliser is something which is added to soil to provide something that it doesn't already have, in order to sustain growth. In the soil you are planted - at home, at work, in your faith or friendships - what fertiliser do you need as you wait in the middle place? What do you not currently have that you sense you need in order to wait well?

What are the weeds which need to be pulled up in order for the new thing to grow? Weeds take nutrients from the ground, strangle growth and take up space. Weeds grow quickly and wildly and are hard to get rid of if you aren't vigilant. Which weeds need to be unearthed - thought patterns or relationships or situations which are draining you of all your resource yet grow too quickly and are hindering your positive growth?

Where does the soil of your life need watering? Where do you feel parched and dry? What does the soil need to be watered with - what would you pour on your life to bring refreshment if you could?

JOURNAL TIME
What fertiliser do you need?
What could be added that you don't already have?

JOURNAL TIME

What weeds could grow here?
(the things that could sap your energy and resources
and strangle the new thing which is trying to grow)

What do you need to pour in to water the ground with?
What will give you refreshment?
How will you do this?

Of course the other thing the seed needs is time. In its season it will grow, not a moment sooner no matter how much work you do on preparing the ground. Some seeds take longer than others to grow, and comparison does not speed the process up. Maybe waiting is the best thing you can do right now. Waiting and weeding, fertilising and watering.

Eden will not grow overnight, neither will the life you dream of; keep going, it doesn't mean it's not on its way.

One of my favourite quotes is from an American church leader named Rick Warren. He says this:

> "When God wants to make a mushroom, he does it overnight, but when He wants to make a giant oak, He takes a hundred years. Great souls are grown through struggles and storms and seasons of suffering. Be patient with the process."

> *'The Purpose Driven Life'* Zondervan, 2007.

You, my friend, are more than a mushroom. What is changing and shifting in you will take some time to produce something great. The space you find yourself in at the moment may be a 'middle' but it is not the end of the story - you are planted, not buried. The threshold you are experiencing may be the best gift you could have, to prepare you for the 'what is to come' that is coming. I doubt the next thing will be all you expect or precisely what you imagine - where would be the fun in that?! I suspect the letting go and the open handedness is what you need to move forward when the time is right. Don't miss what's here, trying to get too quickly to what's next.

The saddest thing about people in the middle is that hurt and unspoken grief causes them to retreat and hide. The thing not to do in the middle is to isolate. When you are stuck in the middle allow those who are stuck in the middle with you into your present reality. Let them into the grief and hope and open-closed hearts. Let them into the mess of the middle and let them be a part of your process. Name the place you are in to them, let them know it's hard and confusing and you don't have answers.

You may need to remind them that it's ok to stay - even good friends sometimes want us to move on a little quickly; then trust them when they see shoots pushing through the soil. You may not notice your new growth as quickly as they do. Let them tell you what they see when that seed starts to do its thing. Who could you invite into the middle with you?

Being stuck in the middle is a gift but not an easy gift. It is a place ripe with goodness if you are one of the brave few who will stop and stay, who will claim they are more than a mushroom so that great oaks can grow and new ground can be claimed. Part of the purpose of man being placed in Eden was to work the ground. It took time and work, every seed in its season, every shoot in its time. Stay present, look around you and soon enough a small shoot will start to appear, new life and new opportunity will begin to break ground.

CHAPTER 13:

STOP AND CELEBRATE...

notice your successes

One of the things we are really bad at in British culture is celebrating success. I'm not sure whether its embarrassment or false humility or simple frugality but we miss out on pausing and cheerleading our achievements. So as we wrap up our conversation about the search for Eden in this format, it is the right thing to do to celebrate our successes.

I said right at the beginning that my greatest hope was that by the end of this book you would feel like you had some tools in your hand to help you build something new in your world. Why? Because I am passionate about people finding spaces they can thrive in. We only have one life here on earth and the idea of people getting to the end of it dissatisfied, unfulfilled and riddled with regret is soul-destroying. We all know the reality that at the end of life, people rarely regret things based on prestige or power, money or titles; in our final breaths. We assess how we loved the people in our world. We assess how we created Eden for ourselves and those who graced our path. Eden is our beginning and it will be our end.

So as we look back at the journey we have taken in this book and the tools we have collected along the way, let's stop and notice all that we have searched for, wrestled with, found out and noticed for the first time. Let's cheerlead where we forgave, loved unconditionally and pioneered new ground.

You are unlikely to see lots of fruit in every area, that would be unrealistic - you may be running, but remember that marathons take a long time to complete! Don't be disheartened, instead celebrate the change you do see and remember that these tools are ones you can take forwards; they are tools to use over and over in order to create a land you love and thrive in. Allow your success in one area to be the voice that cheerleads you on to keep going in the others.

It may be that you can see real change in one of your 'homes' from the relational wheel, it may be that you are standing in hope that you are fertilising ground and praying for something new to grow in its time. Wherever you are, it's worth stopping to notice and celebrate. Let's go through some of the concepts we have looked at in this book and meditate on where you now are in thought, word or deed in your life.

JOURNAL TIME

What does Eden now mean to you in your world?

Where are you sensing a shift in the places you feel welcome or are welcoming others?

What is the next chapter you are beginning to write? How does this differ from the last ones?

JOURNAL TIME

What dream are you seeing become a reality?

Where are you noticing beauty in yourself or others?
How is this changing you or your relationships?

What new ground have you begun to explore?

JOURNAL TIME

How have you reassigned value to a relationship
which was poverty stricken?

How do you notice you are starting to show up more fully?

How do you see you have started to use your voice
rather than silent assumption?

JOURNAL TIME

How have you seen a difference in the areas
which are your blindspots?

What is different in a middle place
that you are currently waiting in?

How do you feel towards the idea of change being
your greatest tool for building healthy relationships?

EPILOGUE:

FIND YOUR TRIBE...

carry on the sacred calling

I think it's time we went back to the fire… remember the place where we started with inky sky and wise counsel? You have been working hard, you have delved into your dreams, your heart, your desire to create something beautiful. You have journeyed long and hard to find new ground and invite others to go to new places with you. You have looked deep into the pool of your own soul to find the reflection of beauty and blindspots, and make the changes that will offer deep connection to those in your world. You have been working deep in the depths.

Remember that this journey began with the circle around the fire. It began when you allowed the stories of others to intertwine with yours, when your voice and theirs started to communicate what you desired to see in your life and relationships.

Remember the voices that called you to tell your story, dream up your home, seek the beauty, pioneer something new. Remember the call to pay the price of love, to come out of hiding, to allow your voice to be heard again. You know to explore your blindspots and stay in the middle places in your relationships. You have the tools and you are using them well.

As you sat around the evening fire you allowed your heart to be opened as you contemplated what Eden could look like for you.

The evening fire remains, the wisdom will continue, but for now there is a call for you to find a new tribe. Building a tribe is a time-honoured calling that many across the centuries and the globe have embarked upon. Tribes are a lifeline when you need a hand or a voice to help guide you back home. You need those two or three people who see the whole you, welcome it all and call you forwards. This is where life change happens.

There are people in your life who have been placed next to you so you can take their hand and lead them towards Eden - you now hold the tools to share with others around the evening fire, offering wisdom and companionship. You placed your running shoes on and you have practiced one step after the other, and now you are starting to find a pace where you are moving forwards to what you desire. You are building something beautiful and others will want to know how you did this. It's time to intentionally find your tribe outside the pages of this book.

As you continue to search and seek and build, I leave you with the challenge to carry on this sacred calling of building a tribe. Who are the two or three you can gather around the evening fire with? Who can you invite in for coffee, or playdates with toddlers and lego, or walks in the hills? Who do you trust to share your heart? Who can you deepen and grow that connection with?

Remember how we talked about 'welcome'? Remember how being welcomed is the tether of acceptance that causes us to throw off 'coping' and truly show up? Offer it to them - the two or three. Welcome them, invest in them, hold space for them as they grow and wrestle as we each have to do.

Love them deeply and wonderfully; and forgive when it goes wonky and the less attractive bits wriggle to the surface. Create a space safe enough for these things to wriggle out and find healing.

It's time to walk on towards Eden, the homes where you are thriving, with those who are in your world.

So stand up, brush the dirt off the seat of your pants and look around you to see the individuals who have been graced into your world for such a time as this. Invite them onto the journey of building spaces where thriving and connection are found. Invite them to hold your hand and your heart as you invite them to search for Eden with you.

Eden is not built overnight, but Eden is being created in you as you live and love in the way you were always intended to, and as you inspire and invite others to do the same.

MY TRIBE

Who are the two or three you are going to invite to be your tribe?

How will you build this tribe well?

SEARCHING FOR EDEN: COACHING CURRICULUM

A UNIQUE PROGRAMME THAT DEEPLY CHANGES THE WAY YOU CONNECT WITH OTHERS IN YOUR WORLD

- *Twelve sessions offering powerful relationship tools*
- *Designed for individuals, couples or small groups*
- *Work with a qualified facilitator for purposeful change*
- *Go to www.helencottee.com for more details*

ABOUT THE AUTHOR

I started my working life in the education system as an English teacher and then worked as a specialist behaviour teacher with young people with life-controlling addictions, severe behavioural issues and anti-social tendencies. I learned to be quick on my feet! But I also learned that everyone has something they can excel at with the right environment, that everyone deserves a second chance and everyone needs someone on their side to champion them in order to succeed.

After having my children, I started working in the non-profit sector leading a team of over 100 paid and volunteer team members in a large faith community. It was here that I developed a passion to raise up and invest in leaders, to create healthy teams and thriving relationships and to help people bring their best to their team.

I published my first book in 2013 called 'Choosing Extraordinary' which is now the material I use as a coach, guiding people to a place of choice in order to live a life they love. The aim of the book was to encourage people to know their dreams and to live according to the things that bring them to life. After the book was released, I began to do keynote talks round the premise of the book and have since spoken widely around the topics of leadership, life fulfilment and personal development. I also speak in faith communities on the impact that your faith can have on your values, dreams and impact on the world.

I am a mentor and teacher on an international theology, leadership and personal development academy holding responsibility for the leadership and personal development arm of the year-long training programme.

After attending a life coaching retreat I fell in love with the tools that coaching offers and the space it creates to usher in life transformation. I was hooked and so trained with CTI to become a co-active life coach and link it with my leadership experience and heart to see people flourish.

I love to communicate through teaching, writing and speaking about the topics I am passionate about. The beauty of coaching is the gift and privilege of creating a longer term relationship with a client - opening up a longer conversation about those same topics that I love and have been championing for over a decade - choosing life and life in all its fullness!

If you would love to work with me more, please get in contact through my website www.helencottee.com

Made in the USA
Charleston, SC
12 June 2016